150 YEARS OF BRAVES TRIVIA

From Boston to Milwaukee to Atlanta

Bradsher Hayes

Perfect Game Publishing,
2022

Copyright @ 2022 Bradsher Hayes
Editor: Gerald Shaw
Book layout by Tiffany Drawdy
Cover Design: Joe Chatman

All rights reserved. No part of this book may be reproduced or utilized in any form or by any means, electronic or mechanical, including photocopying, recording, or by any information storage and retrieval system, except short excerpts for purposes of reviews, without permission in writing from the author.

ISBN: 978-1-7334084-2-4
ISBN: 978-1-7334084-3-1

Printed in the United States of America
Perfect Game Publishing.
First printing August 2022.

In the Memory
of my son
Arthur Bradsher Hayes Jr.

Bo and I saw our only World Series
game together on October 24, 1991.
The Atlanta Braves defeated
The Minnesota Twins in game five 14-5.

It was a memorable night
with the passage of love
for the game of baseball
from father to son.

People ask me what I do in winter when there's no baseball. I'll tell you what I do. I stare out the window and wait for spring.
~Rogers Hornsby

Rogers Hornsby was a player-manager for the Boston Braves in 1928, a season he won the batting title with a .387 average.

A Dedication

*A ballplayer that comes from poverty
gave such riches to the game of baseball
and did so in a noble manner
through an era that dripped with hatred
by some for the Black man.
Hank Aaron helped launch Atlanta
as a big-league city both in sports and culture
and played each game of his career
with style, grace, and consistency.
In the over sixty years, I have carried the love of
the game of baseball in my heart,
I have never seen
a more complete and exceptional player.
In the 150-year history of the Braves,
He was the best to play the game.
Mr. Aaron, this book is dedicated to you.*

INTRODUCTION

I love baseball.

I have been a Braves fan since I was seven years old. One of my most joyful childhood memories was sitting next to the radio with my dad listening to the 1957 World Series when the Milwaukee Braves and New York Yankees battled for the championship. I can still hear Mel Allen's voice crackling through the speaker in my old RCA table radio as he gave the play-by-play.

My dad grew up in Boston. He always talked about the 1914 Fall Classic when his home team upset the mighty Philadelphia Athletics. He and his father were there for the final game to help celebrate the unexpected victory.

My Dad and I were like two peas in a pod. The only thing more remarkable than the love we shared for each other was our lifetime love for baseball and especially the Braves.

My father is the driving force behind this book. He was the one who spoon-fed me questions and answers about the Braves franchise from its roots in 1871 to the move to Milwaukee and how the franchise helped transform Atlanta into a sports town.

After digesting my 489-page historical offering, 150 Years of the Braves, a reader asked if he could borrow my "Cliff Notes." That got me thinking. So here's a condensed version highlighting the most notable moments in the franchise's history. Share in the wealth of knowledge, from the first base hit in Boston in 1871 to the 2021 World Championship celebration.

This is not your ordinary trivia book of one-sentence questions and one-word answers. We've delved more deeply into the storied history and unearthed treasures that will both astound and amuse.

Experience the same joy I felt when I take you around the bases, and you learn the fun facts, discover the oddball moments, and marvel at the individual achievements of the players who made this franchise great.

Read and enjoy. Let 150 Years of Braves Trivia put a twinkle in your eye and bop in your step. Share it with your son. Gift a copy to grandpa. Keep one in your glovebox for road trips. Carry one with you when you go to a doctor's appointment and sit in the waiting room. There are no age restrictions and no prerequisites to enjoy a copy.

The Braves baseball team is the longest-running professional sports franchise in history. Share in their riches.

1871-1952

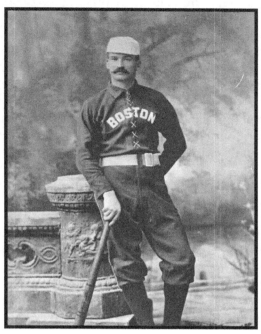

150 Years of Braves Trivia
Boston

1. "Baseball was, is, and always will be the best game in the world." What baseball legend who played for the Braves for one year is credited with this quote?

Answer: Babe Ruth ~ Boston Braves ~ 1935.

2. In 1869, which team was the first to fill their roster with professionals and be led by future Hall of Famer Harry Wright to a perfect 65-0 record and 65-8 the following year?

Answer: The Cincinnati Red Stockings were members of the pioneering National Association of Baseball Players League.

3. The Braves franchise's deepest roots were buried in the National Association. What were the origins of this organization?

Answer: When the Cincinnati Red Stockings folded because of financial concerns after the 1870 season, Wright was hired by businessman Ivers Whitney Adams to help him organize a team for a new league in Boston. Adams was the founder, organizer, and first president of the Boston Baseball Association. Led by the Wright brothers, pitcher and future sporting goods mogul Al Spading, and second baseman Ross Barnes, the Boston Red Stockings won four championships in the first five seasons of the National Association's existence, 1871-1875.

4. What year did the Braves franchise begin playing in the Major Leagues?

Answer: The National League of Professional Baseball was formed in 1876 with an eight-team circuit consisting of the Boston Red Caps, Chicago White Stockings, Cincinnati Red Legs, Hartford Dark Blues, Louisville Grays, Philadelphia Athletics, Brooklyn Mutuals, and St. Louis Browns.

5. Who was the manager of the initial Braves franchise?

Answer: Harry Wright was the first manager when the Braves organization joined the National League in 1876. He would skipper the team from 1876 to 1881, winning the NL pennant in 1877 and 1878. The baseball pioneer, nicknamed and known as the "Father of Professional Baseball," was inducted into the Baseball Hall of Fame in 1953 by the Veterans Committee.

6. The Braves franchise was not always called the Braves. The team was one of the eight members of the new National League in 1876. In its inaugural year, what was the club's name?

Answer: In 1876, the team name was changed from the Boston Red Stockings to the Boston Red Caps to avoid confusion with the new Cincinnati Red Stockings team. With Harry Wright at the team's helm, the Red Caps finished in fourth place of the eight teams in the league's first season. They bounced back and won the pennant in 1877 and 1878.

7. What Hall of Famer got the first hit in the National League and his last hit as a Major Leaguer at age fifty-four?

Answer: On April 22, 1876, Jim O'Rourke smacked the first base hit in the National League's history. O'Rourke captured the NL batting title in 1884 with a .347 average and in his career batted .300 thirteen times and finished with a .310 average. "Orator Jim," as he was nicknamed, played one last game for John McGraw at age fifty-four and got one hit in four at-bats.

8. What player and manager of the Boston franchise between 1876 and 1888 was nicknamed "Honest John" and sometimes was asked to help umpire games he was playing?

Answer: With the Major Leagues having only one umpire on the field and players like King Kelly bending the rules (by cutting across the diamond going from first to third) on the bases, John Morrill, known as "Honest John," was often asked to participate as a second umpire even in games he was a participant.

9. In the second year of its existence, who won the 1877 NL batting title representing the Boston Beaneaters?

Answer: Playing his only season for the 1877 pennant-winning Boston Beaneaters, Deacon White led the NL with a .387 batting average. He also led the NL in seven other offensive categories: hits (103), triples (11), RBI (49), SLG (.545), OPS (.950), OPS+ (193), and TB (145).

10. What Braves pitcher holds the franchise single-season record for shutouts?

Answer: Tommy Bond holds the record with eleven shutouts thrown in 1879. Warren Spahn pitched seven shutouts twice (1947 and 1951). Greg Maddux led the NL with five shutouts (1998) and in four other seasons recorded with three (1994, 1995, 2000, 2001).

11. What Braves pitcher suffered over thirty losses but managed thirty wins in a single season?

Answer: James Evans "Grasshopper Jim" Whitney lost thirty-three games and won thirty contests in his testy 1881 rookie season for the Boston Beaneaters. In his first eight years (five with Boston), Whitney won 187 games.

12. The Red Caps' name would be changed to the Beaneaters in 1883. It would be changed five more times between 1907 and 1941. Can you name four of those teams' nicknames?

Answer: The Red Caps' name was changed to the Beaneaters from 1883 until 1907, when they modified it to the Doves. After altering the title again in 1911 to the Boston Rustlers, the team finally took on the Braves name in 1912. During another brief span between 1936 and 1941, they were called the Bees before changing their name back to the Braves permanently in 1941.

13. Who was this catcher, outfielder, and manager, nicknamed $10,000 Kelly?

Answer: Michael Joseph "King" Kelly was handsome and charismatic. Some say he was the main reason women became attracted to baseball in America. As a member of the Chicago White Stockings, he was annually among the league leaders in most offensive categories. Chicago won five pennants while Kelly played for them. In 1887, Spalding sold Kelly, the National League's most famous player, to the Boston franchise, for the unheard-of sum of $10,000.

14. What ballplayer won forty or more games for the Braves franchise in his first three years?

Answer: No pitcher in Major League history jumped off to a more robust career start than Boston Red Stockings, Irish-born Tommy Bond. In his rookie 1877 season, the gritty five-foot-seven, 160-pound righthander won forty games and lost seventeen with a stellar .702 winning percentage, pitching fifty-eight complete games in as many starts. Bond won forty and forty-three games in the following two seasons.

15. The Boston Beaneaters won back-to-back pennants in 1887 and 1888. Can you name the other two ball clubs that won consecutive pennants and what years they did so?

Answer: The Milwaukee Braves won back-to-back pennants in 1957 and 1958, and the Atlanta Braves in 1991 and 1992, and 1995 and 1996

16. What Braves Hall of Famer was the most prolific leadoff hitter, run-scorer, and base stealer in franchise history?

Answer: There wasn't a base that Billy Hamilton didn't like to steal. "Slidin' Billy" set a record of 117 base thefts that stood for ninety-five years until his record was broken by Lou Brock in 1974. One of the premier leadoff hitters in the game, Hamilton ended his career having scored more runs than the actual games he played in. He scored 1,690 runs in the 1,591 games played. His record of 192 runs scored in 1892 still stands today.

17. Who was this Brown graduate who was a catcher in college that became the first baseman for the best infield quartet in Major League Baseball in the late 1880s?

Answer: Fred Tenney was a rarity. He was one of the few ballplayers to graduate from college, much less a highly regarded university like Brown. After spending three years behind the plate and roaming the outfield, he was moved to first base, joining Bobby Lowe at second base, Herman Long at shortstop, and Jimmy Collins at third base. This talented quartet formed one of the best infields in the history of MLB in the four years they played together for the Boston Beaneaters.

18. His popularity was later compared to Babe Ruth. Who was this beloved ballplayer that thousands of fans paid respects to at his funeral?

Answer: After being traded to the Beaneaters from Chicago, King Kelly became an even bigger star in Boston. A devout following afforded him an expensive home and a horse and carriage. His popularity was later compared to the fans' love for Babe Ruth. In the fall of 1894, Kelly, in a weakened state of health, caught pneumonia and passed away after a brief illness at the tender age of thirty-six. Tens of thousands of fans filed past his casket at his funeral service.

19. What Braves pitcher won forty-nine games and pitched sixty-nine complete games in seventy-two starts in a single season?

Answer: Hall of Famer John Clarkson won 328 in his major league career from 1882 to 1894. In 1889 while pitching for the Braves, he had a 149 and 82 record and pitched sixty-eight complete games in seventy-two starts, giving up 589 hits in 620 innings pitched.

20. In a dead-ball era, he was a pitcher's best friend at third base when the bunt was employed as the deadliest offensive weapon, not the longball. Who was this Brooks Robinson-like, third-sacker of the late 1880s?

Answer: Instead of playing deep at the third base position, Jimmy Collins crept up to the edge of the infield grass. Collins covered a lot of territory at third base. He could make any play in any direction within sixty feet of the bag, not just bunts and ground balls, but also snagged many pop flies in foul territory and short left field.

21. Who threw the first no-hitter in Braves franchise history?

Answer: Jack Stivetts threw the first no-hitter in Braves history on August 6, 1892. Stivetts played eleven seasons in Major League Baseball. He was nicknamed "Happy Jack" due to his pleasant demeanor. He posted twenty or more victories in a season six times. In the year of his no-hitter, he won a career-high thirty-five games.

22. One of the most significant rule changes in MLB occurred in 1893 that greatly affected both hitters and pitchers. What was it?

Answer: The distance from the pitching rubber to home plate was moved back to sixty feet, six inches from a previous distance of fifty feet. The magnitude of the change was reflected in most of the Beaneaters' statistics stepping forward.

23. An immaculate inning occurs when a pitcher strikes out three straight batters on just nine pitches. Who hurled the first immaculate inning in the MLB?

Answer: On June 4, 1889, in the third inning against the Philadelphia Quakers, John Clarkson of the Boston Beaneaters threw only nine pitches and struck out Jim Fogarty, Sam Thompson, and Sid Farrar.

24. Who was the first player in MLB history to reach base three times in one inning?

Answer: On June 18, 1894, Hugh Duffy of the Boston Beaneaters reached base three times in one inning.

25. What Braves twirler won thirty or more games seven times between 1891 and 1898?

Answer: Charles Augustus "Kid" Nichols won thirty-plus games seven times between 1891 and 1898 for the Boston Beaneaters. His career-high wins for the franchise was thirty-five games, achieved in 1892. Kid Nichols had a lifetime W/L record of 362-208 with an ERA of 2.96. Cy Young, Christy Mathewson, Grover Cleveland Alexander, and Warren Spahn were the only pitchers to win more games than Nichols.

26. This Brave played as a Beaneater for nine of his seventeen seasons in the Majors. In 1894, he set the MLB single-season record for batting with a .440 average. Who was this batting champion?

Answer: Hugh Duffy won the Triple Crown in 1894 and led the Beaneaters to four National League titles. Also, he drove in a hundred or more runs eight times. Although only five-feet-seven and weighing only 150 pounds, he led the league in 1894 with eighteen home runs and finished his career with 106.

27. What Braves hit for the highest average in a season, which is still a record in Major League Baseball today?

Answer: In his phenomenal 1894 season, Hugh Duffy batted .440 with 237 hits, sixteen triples, fifty-one doubles, 160 runs scored, 145 RBI, and forty-five stolen bases. His on-base percentage for the year was .502, and his OPS was 1.196 with 374 total bases. Duffy starred in the 1894 World Series, batting .462, going twelve for twenty-seven at the plate, with three doubles, two triples, a home run, and nine RBI.

28. Who was the first player in the Major League to hit four home runs in a single game?

Answer: Bobby Lowe hit four homers for the Boston Beaneaters against the Cincinnati Reds and Icebox Chamberlain on May 30, 1894. In two of his four historic swings, he connected for two of his home runs over the left-field fence in the third inning. He blasted his third four-bagger in the fifth inning and finished his longball barrage, joining his keystone partner, Herman Long, in back-to-back homers in the sixth. Long capped his day with a single in the seventh, earning him a record seventeen total bases for his afternoon's work.

29. This duo played four years for the Beaneaters between 1892 and 1895, helping the Braves franchise win two pennants. They left many records in their wake and were affectionately dubbed "The Heavenly Twins." Who were these two Hall of Famers?

Answer: Hugh Duffy and his outfield sidekick, Tommy McCarthy, led the Beaneaters to two league championships in four years. They were the strongest outfield tandem in baseball. In 1893 the two led the league in hitting, showcasing .363 and .346, respectively. On the defensive side, the two combined for fifty-five assists in the outfield in 1894. "The Heavenly Twins" formed a clever twosome on offense. They were adept at executing the hit-and-run. The two outfielders were even ahead of their time when it came to contract negotiations. They held out jointly, just as Dodger pitchers Sandy Koufax and Don Drysdale did some seven decades later.

30. This Boston Beaneater, in the Hall of Fame, only played six of his thirteen seasons in Boston, but drove in a hundred runs two seasons in a row (1893-1894) with them. Who was the right fielder who was linked by the press with Hugh Duffy as the "Heavenly Twins"?

Answer: Tommy McCarthy is linked in baseball lore with the introduction of the hit-and-run technique, the fake bunt and the double steal. With the St. Louis Browns from 1888 to 1891, he scored over a hundred runs each season and batted .350 with ninety-five runs in 1891.

31. Hank Aaron holds ten Braves franchise records, including most career hits, doubles, and best single-season slugging percentage. What Brave that played in the nineteenth century holds eight?

Answer: Hugh Duffy, who played for the Braves in the years 1892-1896, holds eight records, including the highest single-season batting average (.440) and the best single-season slugging percentage (.694). Duffy also holds the record for most season hits (237), RBI (145), runs (161), doubles (fifty-one), total bases (374), and OPS (1.196).

32. What team in the Braves' 150-year franchise history had the highest winning percentage for a single season?

Answer: After a three-year downslide, the 1897 Beaneaters posted a 93-39-3 record and won the National League pennant, their fourth of the decade and seventh in franchise history. The team's .705 winning percentage has never been bettered.

33. What Braves pitcher was the leader in the National League for three consecutive years (1896-1898) and was inducted into the MLB Hall of Fame in 1949?

Answer: Kid Nichols was a pitcher with the Boston Beaneaters for twelve seasons before the turn of the twentieth century. He was the NL wins leader for three consecutive years, winning thirty or more games in each of those seasons and amassing a 361-208 career record with 1,873 strikeouts. He was inducted into baseball's Hall of Fame in 1949 and into the Braves Hall of Fame in 2004.

34. Known for his sweeping curveball, who is this hurler who holds the modern-day record for forty-five complete games?

Answer: Victor Gazaway Willis holds the modern National League record for complete games (forty-five in 1902) and losses (twenty-nine in 1905) in a season playing for the Beaneaters. The twenty-two-year-old rookie led the Beaneaters to a pennant with a 25-13 record. In his next season, the Boston workhorse used his sweeping curveball to pitch the second no-hitter in franchise history, beating Washington, 7-1. After his rookie season, he had seven more twenty-game seasons, three with Boston. He was inducted into the Baseball Hall of Fame in 1995.

35. Who was the first manager in Braves history to win 1,000 or more games?

Answer: Manager Frank Selee had 1,004 wins from 1890 to 1901 for the Braves franchise. In his twelve years leading the Beaneaters, his teams won five pennants, and three runner-up finishes.

36. Who was this Boston Beaneater shortstop that made more errors (1,096) than any shortstop in the National League's history, but he also made plays most never dreamed of?

Answer: Most argued that Herman Long attempting circus catches and stabbing balls deep in the hole resulted in more miscues. Many consider him the best shortstop to play in the nineteenth century. He led Boston to five pennants between 1891 and 1898. He and second-baseman Bobby Lowe were the only everyday players to be part of all five pennant winners.

37. True or False: At one time, the Atlanta Braves were known as the Boston Doves?

Answer: True. The franchise changed its name from the Boston Beaneaters, owned by Arthur Soden, when the team was sold to the Dovey Brothers in 1907.

38. Why was the Boston ball club of 1912 first called the Braves?

Answer: William Russell bought the franchise before the 1911 season and named the club the Rustlers. After one season, the team was sold to James Gaffney, an alderman for Tammany Hall, which used an Indian headdress for its emblem and referred to its members as Braves. Consequently, the franchise became known as the Braves for the first time in 1912. Former star pitcher John Montgomery Ward and two former high-ranking policemen were involved in 1912 to rename the team from the Rustlers to the Braves.

39. *In 1912 the Boston Braves and the New York Giants set modern-day records for runs and stolen bases. Can you give more details?*

Answer: In a contest that New York won, 21-12, over Boston, the Giants stole eleven bases and the Braves and Giants combined for seventeen runs in the ninth inning.

40. Who was this honorary second baseman that was traded to the Braves and was nicknamed the "Human Crab?"

Answer: At five-feet-six, 125 pounds, Johnny Evers pound for pound was the toughest player in MLB. His combative play and his fights with umpires earned him the nickname "The Human Crab." He frequently argued with umpires and received numerous suspensions during his career. He was known to push his teammates to a higher level of play. "They claim he is a crab, and perhaps they are right," Cleveland Indians manager Joe Birmingham once observed. "But I would like to have twenty-five such crabs playing for me. If I did, I would have no doubts over the pennant. They would win hands down."

41. Why was the franchise nicknamed the "Miracle Braves?"
Answer: The 1914 Boston Braves pulled off one of the most amazing come-from-behind from last-to-first baseball finishes in the history of MLB, earning them the name the "Miracle Braves." Mired in last place at mid-season, the resurgent Braves won the pennant by ten and a half games over the New York Giants. The never-quit ball club swept the heavily-favored Philadelphia Athletics in 1914 for the first franchise World Series Championship.

42. Who was the catcher for the 1914 Braves that was one of the biggest stars in the 1914 World series?

Answer: Hank Gowdy came out swinging in the Fall Classic. He had a .545 batting average, which included the only home run of the series plus a triple, three doubles, and a single in the historic upset of Connie Mack's Philadelphia Athletics. In October after the series, Gowdy returned to his hometown of Columbus, Ohio, where he had fifty thousand fans celebrate him in a parade.

43. What Braves hurler won nineteen of his last twenty pitching decisions in a season and led his team to a pennant in 1914?

Answer: Bill James was an integral member of the Braves team that went from last place, 11½ back in July, to win the pennant by 10½ games. From July 9 until the end of the season, he went 19-1 with a 1.51 ERA. His only setback came on August 22 in Pittsburgh when he lost, 3-2, in twelve innings. Without that defeat, James would have ended his year with a record-breaking twenty-game winning streak.

44. He led his team from last place in July to first place and the World Series in September. Who is this National League manager who was called the "Miracle Man?"

Answer: The always impeccably dressed manager George Stallings led the 1914 Boston Braves from last place in mid-July to the National League championship and a World Series sweep of the powerful Philadelphia Athletics–resulting in a nickname he would bear for the rest of his life: "The Miracle Man."

45. Who was the franchise's first player to win the National League Most Valuable Player Award?

Answer: Second baseman Johnny Evers was there in 1914. After making his name as one of the famous double-play combination players earlier for the Cubs, Evers was in his first season with the Braves in 1914. In close balloting, he won the Chambers Award over teammates Rabbit Maranville and Bill James.

46. What newcomer to the Braves franchise was runner-up to Johnny Evers for the 1914 MVP?

Answer: Rabbit Maranville finished third in the MVP voting in his first full season, playing for the Boston Braves as a twenty-one-year-old in 1913, even though his batting average was just .247 in 143 games with two homers. The following year, Maranville was the runner-up in the MVP voting to teammate Johnny Evers.

47. The Braves franchise has had seven players that have been selected as the most valuable player in the National League. Who was the first?

Answer: Johnny Evers, traded to the Beaneaters from Chicago the year before, was selected as the Most Valuable Player in the National League in 1914. He won the Chambers Award as the NL MVP., with teammates Rabbit Maranville and Bill James placing second and third in the voting.

48. What new stadium in Boston was the talk of Major League Baseball in 1915?

Answer: Braves Field was the first ballpark to seat more than forty thousand fans. A single deck of eighteen thousand covered seats extended around home plate and down both foul lines. The ballpark was built with the deepest fence dimensions in MLB.

49. Ty Cobb visited this stadium and commented, "Nobody will ever hit a ball out of this park." What ballpark was he referring to?

Answer: The stadium was home to the Boston Braves of the National League from 1915 to 1952. Original dimensions at Braves Field were 402 feet (left), 550 feet (center), and 402 feet (right), leading to many inside-the-park home runs. The field was surrounded by a ten-foot wall. Cobb was partially right because of its extraordinarily deep fences; the first home run in Braves Field was not hit until New York Giants catcher Frank Snyder cleared the left field fence just inside the foul pole with a longball in 1922.

50. What Boston Braves journeyman hurled twenty shutout innings before taking a 2-0 loss in the twenty-first?

Answer: Pitching a complete game was common practice for Braves hurler Art Nehf. By the end of the season, he would lead the league by going the distance on twenty-eight occasions. For twenty innings the Braves' hard-luck loser matched goose eggs with two Pirate pitchers, only to surrender two runs in the twenty-first stanza and take the loss. His team stranded nineteen baserunners in the contest.

51. Who was this two-sport professional athlete who also won two Olympic medals and played for the Boston Braves in 1918?

Answer: The Associated Press ranked Jim Thorpe as the "greatest athlete" from the first fifty years of the twentieth century. Thorpe won two gold medals in the 1912 Olympics (pentathlon and the decathlon). In the last year of his Major League career, he played a portion of the season for the Braves, batting .327 over sixty games. He also started for the Canton Bulldogs football team, leading them to three professional championships.

52. What was the longest extra-inning contest ever played by a Braves team?

Answer: The longest game by innings in Major League Baseball was a 1-1 tie in the National League between the Boston Braves and the Brooklyn Robins in twenty-six innings, at Braves Field in Boston on May 1, 1920. Boston's Joe Oeschger hurled the entire twenty-six innings of the contest. "If a pitcher couldn't go the distance," Oeschger would comment to the *Sarasota Herald-Tribune* decades later, "he soon found himself in some other form of occupation."

53. What are the most pitches thrown in one game? Was it 375, 475, 575, or 675?

Answer: Leon Cadore of the Brooklyn Dodgers is likely to have pitched every inning of a twenty-six-inning game in 1920, which would be the

MLB record. During the course of the game, he is estimated to have thrown 360 pitches. Joe Oeschger of the Boston Braves also pitched all twenty-six innings and threw an estimated 319 during the game, making the total for both hurlers 679 pitches.

54. Who was this future Hall of Fame pitcher that returned to baseball in 1923 as part owner and team president of the Boston Braves?

Answer: One of the few highlights during the dismal 1920s decade of the Braves was the return to baseball by Christy Mathewson. Although initial plans called for Mathewson to be principal owner and team president of the Boston Braves, his health had deteriorated so much that he could perform only nominal duties. He turned over the presidency to Emil Fuchs after the season.

55. In their 150-year history, what Brave player has stolen home the most times in a single game?

Answer: Doc Gautreau stole home twice in an eleven-inning victory over the Brooklyn Robins on September 3, 1927, joining four other National Leaguers, including Honus Wagner and Joe Tinker, in accomplishing the remarkable feat. The five-foot-four, 129-pound Gautreau scored three of the four runs in the contest.

56. What player is the career record holder for the most triples by a Brave?

Answer: Rabbit Maranville, whose career spanned from 1913 to 1935, had 103 triples as a member of the Braves. He also collected 380 two-base hits.

57. Who was this Brave who always seemed to be where the ball was and made more putouts than other shortstop in the Major Leagues?

Answer: Rabbit Maranville is the all-time leader in career putouts as a shortstop with 5,139. Maranville is the only shortstop to record more than 5,000 career putouts.

58. What Hall of Famer and seven-time batting champion played for and managed the Braves for one year, but was traded away for an astronomical sum of $200,000 and five players one year later?

Answer: Rogers Hornsby, nicknamed "the Rajah," joined and starred for the Braves for one season in 1928. On May 23, with the team off to a dismal start, manager Jack Slattery resigned, and Hornsby took over the club in a player/manager capacity. The team floundered under Hornsby. Regardless of the circumstances, though, Hornsby could hit. He won the National League Batting Crown at .387, a modern-day record. After the season, in which the Braves fished 44 ½ games out of first place, the tempestuous Hornsby was traded to the Cubs for $200,000 and five players. It was his fourth team in four years.

59. Frustrated with the team's managerial debacle and a dismal seventh-place finish and record of 50–103, 44½ games behind the St. Louis Cardinals, what major step did owner Emil Fuchs make to try to remedy the bleak situation?

Answer: Coming off an abysmal 1928 season, owner Judge Emil Fuchs made the decision to manage his own team for the following season. He finished in eighth place in NL standings with a 56-98 record.

60. The 1920s was a dismal decade for the Braves. Their record was 603-1531 for the ten seasons and they had one twenty-game winner. Who was he?

Answer: Joe Oeschger posted a 20-14 record in 1921, leading the league with three shutouts. In his twelve-year career, the hurler would never win more than fifteen games.

61. Baseball historian Lee Allen described this Braves skipper as follows, "he managed to finish fourth or fifth with teams that should have been eighth." Who is this Hall of Fame field general?

Answer: Bill McKechnie was the first manager to win World Series titles with two teams (1925 Pittsburgh Pirates and 1940 Cincinnati Reds). He remains one of only two field generals to win pennants with three teams, capturing the National League title in 1928 with the St. Louis Cardinals. His sixth-place finish and record of 70-84 in his first year were vast improvements over their previous two seasons, when they posted records of 50-103 and 56-98, placing them seventh and eighth respectively. In 1932 McKechnie led the Braves to a 77-77 season, and in 1933 Boston enjoyed their first winning season in thirteen years, recording an 83-71 record and finishing in second place. The wheels came off in 1935 with the addition of Babe Ruth to the team and a weak pitching staff that had one starter win eleven games.

62. Of the eighteen players who started the 1934 All-Star Game who was the only player not elected to the Baseball Hall of Fame?

Answer: Wally Berger of the Boston Braves. The starters in the All-Star Game in both leagues were as follows: American League: Charlie Gehringer (2B), Heinie Manush (LF), Babe Ruth (RF), Lou Gehrig (1B), Jimmy Fox (3B), Al Simmons (CF), Joe Rosen (SS), Bill Dickey (C), Lefty Gomez (P). National League starters: Frankie Frisch (2B), Pie Traynor (3B), Joe Medwick (OF), Kiki Cuyler (OF), Wally Berger (OF), Bill Terry (1B), Travis Jackson (SS), Gabby Hartnett (C), Carl Hubbell (P).

63. Who was the first player for the Braves to hit thirty or more home runs in consecutive seasons?

Left to Right Babe Ruth, Wally Berger

Answer: Wally Berger hit thirty-five home runs for the Braves in 1934 and thirty-four longballs in 1935.

64. What famous New York Yankee legend ended his career with the Braves?

Answer: Babe Ruth began his historic career with the Boston Red Sox in 1914 (American League) and ended his playing days with the Boston Braves (National League) in 1935, a year he finished with only six home runs. He hit three homers in his last full game played and retired one week later on May 30, 1935.

65. When Rabbit Maranville hung up his spikes in 1935, he was the longest-tenured ballplayer in MLB, having played for twenty-three seasons. His record stood for fifty-one years. Who broke his record?

Answer: Pete Rose was the 1963 Rookie of the Year and played twenty-four seasons, breaking Rabbit Maranville's record that stood for five decades. He retired in 1986 after collecting 4,256 base hits.

66. What was the worst season in the Braves franchise history?

Answer: The Boston Braves 1935 season was a disaster. The pitching-poor ball club finished in eighth place and a whopping sixty-one and a half games behind the pennant-winning Chicago Cubs. It was the worst record in the National League and the Majors.

67. Who would be the last pitcher in the twentieth century to lose at least twenty-five games in one season?

Answer: Two years after posting a 20-10 record, Braves pitcher Ben Cantwell suffered through a disastrous 4-25 year in 1935 with an ERA of 4.61. The thirty-three-year-old would strike out only thirty-four batters in forty-nine games. He would be the last pitcher in the twentieth century to lose at least twenty-five games in one season

68. After suffering the worst record in modern-day NL history, Boston changed the franchise's name for the sixth time. What was their new name for the ballclub?

Answer: After a dismal 1935 and owner Fuchs' financial woes, the MLB took control of the team and allowed a sale to a new owner. In an effort to shed new light on a losing ball club, new owner Bob Quinn polled the fanbase and renamed his ball club the Bees in 1936. The name would stick for five years. The franchise would settle on the Braves' name in 1941 on a permanent basis.

69. Where was the first All-Star Game that the Braves franchise hosted?

Answer: The 1936 Summer Classic was played at Braves Field with 25,556 fans in attendance. The NL edged the AL, 4-2, for their first win in All-Star Game history. Wally Berger of the Braves was on the second squad but did not play in the event.

70. Two rookies stepped into MLB in a Bees (Braves franchise) uniform in 1937 and achieved something as a twosome that had never been done before or since?

Answer: When thirty-three-year-old Jim Turner and thirty-year-old Lou Fette, both right-handers, took the mound for their first appearances for Boston, the first words out of the fans' mouths were, "Who are these guys?" By October, these rookies were the talk of the city and the entire

National League. The two had won twenty games for the weakest offensive team in baseball and both pitched five shutouts for the year. Only two other National League pitchers won twenty games in 1937. The sensational Carl Hubbell and rookie left-handed Cliff Melton both hurled for the pennant-winning Giants.

71. What Bees/Braves manager finished seventh in four of his six years but won ten pennants as the New York Yankees manager?

Answer: Many baseball fans know Casey Stengel as the New York Yankees manager who won ten pennants and seven World Series championships. Others may recall the man nicknamed late in his career "the professor" that skippered the Mets for four years. At the start of a career, every manager has to pay his dues to gain experience. Casey Stengel led Boston to a fifth-place finish and a 77-75 record in his first year with the Bees in 1938. His clubs finished in seventh place for the next four years.

72. What Braves catcher, one of the heroes of the 1914 World Series, was the only Major League player to serve his country in World War I and World War II?

Answer: Hank Gowdy was an American hero on and off the playing field. On June 1, 1917, Gowdy became the first active Major League player who enlisted in the Army, joining the Ohio National Guard to serve on the battlefield during WWI. Gowdy served with distinction in the famed Rainbow Division, so named by General Pershing. In 1942, the fifty-two-year-old volunteered again for military service. He returned to Fort Benning, commissioned a captain, where he oversaw the Army's physical education program.

73. Only two Major League pitchers have hit three homers in a single game. Can you name the Braves pitcher who accomplished this extraordinary feat?

Answer: Big Jim Tobin hit three home runs for the Boston Braves on May 13, 1942, in a 6-5 victory. Incidentally, the previous day, manager Casey Stengel called on Tobin to pinch-hit, and he responded with a homer. For the 1942 season, Tobin led the league in complete games and innings pitched while recording twelve wins and twenty-one loses. Tobin ended the season with six home runs.

74. What future Hall of Famer left the Boston Braves as a twenty-two-year-old to serve his country in the military and receive the Purple Heart and Bronze Star for injuries and bravery in combat?

Answer: Warren Spahn entered military service on December 3, 1942, after pitching in only four games in his MLB career. Spahn saw action in the brutal Battle of the Hürtgen Forest and the Battle of the Bulge. He received wounds in defense of the Ludendorff Railroad Bridge at Remagen, and for his bravery, he received a Purple Heart and Bronze Star.

75. What Braves pitcher threw the fewest pitches ever in a Major League complete game?

Answer: On August 10, 1944, Red Barrett threw an economical and record-setting fifty-eight pitches to dispose of his former team, the Cincinnati Reds, in a 2-0 nine-inning shutout and facing twenty-nine batters. He allowed two hits and didn't walk or strike out a batter. The contest was the shortest night game in Major League history, the game lasting seventy-five minutes.

76. What Boston Braves player broke Rogers Hornsby's thirty-three game hitting streak that left him near the top of the league in hitting at the end of the year?

Answer: Tommy Holmes had a thirty-seven-game hitting streak in 1945 between June 6 and July 8. During the streak, he batted .423 and at the season's end placed second in the league in hitting with a .352 average. When it comes to the NL, only Pete Rose's forty-four-game hit streak is longer than the thirty-seven-gamer by Holmes.

77. This future Brave lettered in four sports at Union-Endicott High School in New York and received scholarship offers for football to Syracuse, Colgate, Duke, and Notre Dame. Who was this star athlete and where did he attend college?

Answer: Star-athlete Johnny Logan graduated from high school in January 1945. His athletic career was promptly put on hold. "I went into the Army right out of high school," he was quoted as saying. "I was drafted." Upon returning from the war, the offers from the big colleges dried up. Logan attended an extension college in Endicott, before the Braves signed him to a $2,500 contract, $1,500 of which he gave to his parents.

78. In his inaugural season with Boston he won the MVP. Who was this Braves third baseman?

Answer: Bob Elliott, nicknamed, "Mr. Team," won the N.L. MVP in 1947 hitting twenty-two home runs, with 113 RBI's and a .317 batting average.

79. Of 1,000 ballplayers ranked with strikeouts per hundred at-bats, this Boston Brave ranks fourth-lowest. Who is this hitter with a keen eye?

Answer: Tommy Holmes had an eagle eye when it came to hitting and knowing the strike zone. In 5,566 plate appearances (4,992 official at-bats), he struck out a measly 122 times.

80. Who was the first Brave pitcher ever to hit a home run on his way to pitching a no-hitter?

Answer: In 1944, against the Dodgers at Braves Field, Jim Tobin needed only ninety-eight pitches and an hour and a half to pitch the big leagues' first no-hitter since St. Louis Cardinal Lon Warneke's in 1941. He also smacked one of his seventeen (thirteen for the Braves) career home runs.

81. He was the last hurler to pitch against Babe Ruth and the first pitcher to face Jackie Robinson in his inaugural MLB at-bat. Who was this All-Star hurler who many deemed the best pitcher in baseball between 1946 and 1950?

Answer: In a Red Cross benefit game in Yankee Stadium on July 28, 1943, Johnny Sain faced a forty-eight-year-old Ruth, who left his third-base coaching duties for one last at-bat. Sain's catcher advised him not to embarrass Ruth in his old stomping grounds and not throw him any curveballs. After a towering drive that went foul, Ruth walked on five pitches in his last-ever time at the plate in an organized game. Sain was the first Major-League pitcher to face Robinson and held Jackie hitless in his first three trips to the plate. In the seventh inning, after Sain walked the Dodger rookie, Robinson scored the go-ahead run in a 5-3 Dodger comeback win. It would be Sain's first loss of the season.

82. Who was the first Brave inductee into the National Baseball Hall of Fame?

Answer: Hugh Duffy, who played for the Beaneaters between 1892 and 1900, was chosen by the Old-Timers Committee for the class of 1945. Duffy's career as a player, coach, manager, executive, and team owner, spanned sixty-eight years. His batting average of .440 in 1894 is a record many fans feel will never be broken.

83. What Braves player returned from three years of military service in 1946 and won twenty games in four of his first five years playing full seasons?

Answer: John Sain, pitching alongside Warren Spahn who had also served three years in the military, stormed into the National League scene winning twenty games in four out of his five years since coming back. His best year was 1948 when he was the runner-up for the National League's Most Valuable Player Award in the Braves' pennant-winning season of 1948, after leading the National League in wins, complete games, and innings pitched.

84. What Hall of Fame manager led the St. Louis Cardinals to three pennants before skippering the Boston Braves into the World Series in 1948?

Answer: Boston was in desperate need of a manager who could bring winning results. Owner Lou Perini started from the top. He enticed baseball's best skipper at that time, Billy Southworth, with a record contract offer of $30,000 a year. Boston captured the 1948 pennant six-and-a-half games ahead of St. Louis, the team Southworth had managed to a World Series victory in 1944. It was the franchise's first championship flag and a trip to the World Series since the "Miracle Braves" of 1914.

85. What Boston Brave hit the most home runs in the team's history?

Answer: Wally Berger hit 199 home runs for the Braves, including thirty-eight in his 1930 debut season.

86. The Braves have had eight players in their franchise awarded the Rookie of the Year Award. Who was the first player in Braves franchise history to win this award?

Answer: Alvin Ralph Dark, nicknamed "Blackie" and "The Swamp Fox," was a shortstop and manager. He played fourteen years for five National League teams from 1946 through 1960. Dark was named the Major League's 1948 Rookie of the Year after batting .322 for the Boston Braves. Other Braves winners of the award are Sam Jethroe (1950), Earl Williams (1971), Bob Horner (1978), David Justice (1990), Rafael Furcal (2000), Craig Kimbrel (2011), and Ronald Acuña Jr. (2018).

87. It's been almost seven decades since the famed rhyme "Spahn and Sain and Pray for Rain" was introduced into popular culture. Can you recite the entire Braves rhyme and explain it?

Answer: The Braves were in the thick of a pennant race and were short-handed for pitching. Warren Spahn and Johnny Sain were being depended on to carry the load. On a rainy day, a bored sportswriter came up with this appropriate-for-the-time lyric.

> First, we'll use Spahn,
> Then we'll use Sain,
> Then an off day,
> Followed by rain.
> Back will come Spahn
> Followed by Sain
> And followed,
> We Hope,
> By two days of rain.

The poem appeared in the wake of a four-day gap (September 7-10) when no games were played, more than likely the result of inclement weather. With no games to write about, sportswriters often wax creative.

88. In the 1948 World Series, the Boston Braves would face the oldest rookie ever to pitch in MLB. Who was this ageless wonder and how old was he?

Answer: At forty-two years of age, Satchel Paige appeared for the Indians, becoming the first black pitcher to take the mound in World Series history. He pitched a perfect two-thirds of an inning and was credited with the win.

89. She attended her first baseball game in Beantown as a thirteen-year-old with her father. Who was this person that became known as the greatest Boston baseball fan that ever lived?

Answer: When Lolly Hopkins was entering her teens, her father began taking her to games. The two would take the fifty-mile train ride into Boston and attend games at both South End Grounds (Beaneaters/Braves) and the Huntington Avenue Grounds (Red Sox). They chose not to pick a favorite between the two teams. Whichever ball club was in Boston on her father's day off would determine the ticket he would buy. A fellow

fan gave her a megaphone to cheer the Braves and Red Sox on. She was a loyal fan, with her megaphone always with her for over fifty years, attending as many as three games a week.

90. What player for the Braves became the first rookie to hit three home runs in a single game?

Answer: Eddie Mathews, the twenty-year-old rookie, hit three home runs in the last game the Braves would ever play in Boston on September 27, 1952, giving him a total of twenty-five for the year. Mathews ended the 1952 campaign with a disappointing fifty-three RBIs and 113 strikeouts. The remainder of his career showed a huge improvement in his numbers. The 1953 season would mark the first year with his new franchise in Milwaukee, where Mathews would homer thirty or more times for nine straight years.

91. What player broke the color barrier with the Boston Braves in 1950?

Answer: Sam Jethroe was the first Black ballplayer in the city of Boston and won the Rookie of the Year Award with the Braves in 1950. He'd tried out for the Boston Red Sox at Fenway Park in 1945, with Jackie Robinson and Marvin Williams, but the Red Sox passed on them. The Red Sox signed Pumpsie Green in 1959, making them the last team to desegregate in MLB. Robinson went on to break the Major-League color barrier and won Rookie of the Year in 1947.

92. What Braves hurler pitched alongside Warren Spahn with the Boston Braves in the 1940s and became one of baseball's pre-eminent pitching coaches in the 1960s-1980s?

Answer: Between 1946 and 1950, Johnny Sain won twenty games four times, but most do not know of his contributions as a pitching coach. After his playing career, he achieved unparalleled success as a coach with six Major League teams. Sixteen of the pitchers he mentored won twenty games in a season. After his stints with the Yankees, in which he coached Whitey Ford to twenty-five wins in 1961 and twenty-four in 1963, he moved on to Minnesota and transformed a mediocre staff into a 1965 American League pennant winner. The next stop was Detroit where he guided Denny McLain to two Cy Young Awards. With Chicago from 1970 to 1975, Sain built a strong pitching staff, and he finished his career from 1985 to 1988, mentoring the young Leo Mazzone on the finer points of pitching.

93. In 1947 Bob Feller led the American League with five shutouts. Who was the leader in the National League?

Answer: Warren Spahn hurled seven shutouts to lead the National League. All-Star teammate Johnny Sain pitched three.

94. What Milwaukee star slugger improved his hitting skills after school with his mother throwing batting practice and his father shagging fly balls?

Answer: Eddie Mathews talked about his parents helping him be a better ballplayer in his Hall of Fame induction speech. "My mother used to pitch to me and my father would shag balls. If I hit one up the middle close to my mother, I'd have some extra chores to do. My mother was instrumental in making me a pull hitter."

95. In 2007 the most complete games pitched in the Majors was seven. This Braves pitcher had twenty-eight complete games in 1948. What Braves pitcher had a September to remember hurling nine complete games in twenty-nine days?

Answer: In the nine games Johnny Sain pitched in September 1948, he pitched a nine-inning game in each outing and won seven times. Sain had twenty-four wins for the year and twenty-eight complete games, leading the Braves to the National League pennant.

96. After Jackie Robinson won the inaugural Rookie of the Year, who was the second Black player to receive this prestigious award?

Answer: Sam Jethroe of the Milwaukee Braves won the award in 1950. At age thirty-two, he was the oldest ball player to ever receive the Rookie of the Year award. The Milwaukee speedster, nicknamed "The Jet," scored a hundred runs and led the league with thirty-five stolen bases.

97. When the Braves left Boston after their eighty-one-year run, how many pennants had they captured?

Answer: They left Boston with nine pennants. The Red Caps/Beaneaters were one of the league's dominant teams during the nineteenth century, winning a total of eight pennants. The Boston Braves won pennants in 1914 and 1948. The one World Series championship was captured by the "Miracle Braves" in 1914.

1953-1965

150 Years of Braves Trivia
Milwaukee

98. Thirteen MLB teams have relocated to different cities since 1902. Can you name the third that was the first to change venues in five decades?

Answer: When the Boston Braves lost the attendance battle with the Boston Red Sox, owner Lou Perrini moved the ball club to Milwaukee. This was the first relocation since the New York Yankees after leaving the city of Baltimore, where their franchise was formed in 1901.

99. What was the first fair ball hit in Milwaukee County Stadium?

Answer: St Louis Cardinal Stan Musial singled to right field against starter Warren Spahn.

100. The Milwaukee Braves won their first-ever home game in County Stadium in ten innings. Who were the heroes?

Answer: Bill Bruton started his Major League career in 1953, the first year the Braves moved its franchise to Milwaukee. On April 14 of that year, his tenth-inning home run gave the Braves a 3–2 victory over the Cardinals in Milwaukee's first Major League game. Warren Spahn earned the win with an impressive ten-inning outing, allowing six hits.

101. Which of these players wasn't playing for Milwaukee in 1953: Joe Adcock, Johnny Logan, Red Schoendienst, Mel Roach?

Answer: Red Schoendienst joined the Braves during the 1957 season. He placed third in the MVP voting for the year and helped propel the Braves into the World Series.

102. He was the only Wisconsin native on the Milwaukee Braves in their inaugural season. He started in the first game at Milwaukee County Stadium on April 3, 1953. Nicknamed "Handy Andy," who was this popular player?

Answer: Andy Pafko was known for good hitting and fielding and contributed to championship-caliber teams in three different cities. In his first year with Milwaukee, the Wisconsin native batted .297, scoring seventy runs while collecting 153 hits, seventeen home runs, and seventy-two RBIs. His keen eye prevented him from swinging at bad pitches, and he struck out only thirty-three times in 516 at-bats.

103. What Braves player hit two bases-loaded triples in the same game?

Answer: On August 2, 1959, Bill Bruton hit two bases-loaded triples in one game. The feat had only been accomplished once before (Elmer Valo, 1949) and has only been achieved a single time since (Duane Kuiper, 1978).

104. Who was the youngest player in National League history to hit forty-five or more home runs in a single season?

Answer: Eddie Mathews was only twenty-one when hit forty-seven home runs in 1953.

105. Of the players that had been with the team thirteen years or more, he and Chipper Jones are the only players to spend their entire career with the organization. Who is this jack-of-all-trades who played seven positions with the Braves?

Answer: Sebastian Daniel "Sibbi" Sisti played seven different positions with the team. He was a fan favorite because of his perseverance and willingness to contribute whenever his manager needed him. Joining the team as an eighteen-year-old, Sisti played for the Braves for thirteen seasons from 1939 until his retirement in 1953.

106. From 1911 until 1963, only four players hit home runs into the Polo Grounds centerfield bleachers. Two of them were Braves. Can you name them?

Answer: Milwaukee first baseman Joe Adcock's mammoth drive reached the dead-center bleachers at the Polo Grounds on April 29, 1953, traveling over 485 feet, an occurrence that had never been done before. Hammerin' Hank Aaron, his teammate in 1955, was the second to accomplish this extraordinary feat.

107. In 1954, during spring training in Bradenton, Florida, Black players were barred from rooming in the same motel as their white teammates. Where did they stay?

Answer: Henry Aaron, Charlie White, Billy Bruton, and Wes Covington lived in an apartment over a garage owned by schoolteacher Lulu Gibson.

108. What famous hitter suffered an injury in the spring training of 1954 that gave Hank Aaron a spot in the Braves lineup?

Bobby Thomson (L), Hank Aaron (R)

Answer: A broken ankle suffered by hard-hitting Bobby Thomson opened the door for Aaron to step into the Braves lineup.

109. What Milwaukee speedster led the National League in stolen bases for three consecutive years in the early fifties?

Answer: Billy Bruton, in his first three years with the Milwaukee Braves, led the NL with twenty-six, thirty-four, and twenty-five thefts between 1953 and 1955.

110. "I've only known three or four perfect swings in my time. This lad has one of them." Who made this comment, and who was he referring to?

Answer: The holder of the highest career batting average in the history of MLB, Ty Cobb, made this comment about Eddie Mathews.

111. This Braves Hall of Famer set a record of eighteen total bases in a single game. This achievement held up for forty-four years before it was broken in 2002. Who was this Braves slugger?

Answer: Joe Adcock hit four home runs and a (near-miss fifth home run) double, giving him eighteen total bases. In the same contest, Eddie Mathews hit two longballs and Andy Pafko had a solo blast. Adcock's record was broken on May 23, 2002, by Shawn Green of the Los Angeles Dodgers. Green also hit four home runs, double and single, and ended with nineteen total bases.

112. What Braves player was on the cover of the first issue of Sports Illustrated?

Answer: Eddie Mathews graced the first cover of *Sports Illustrated*. The magazine released its inaugural issue on August 16, 1954. The cover photo, taken by Mark Kauffman, features Milwaukee Braves great Eddie Mathews taking a swing with County Stadium towering in the background. Catcher Wes Westrum and umpire Augie Donatelli are also in the image. There was no article about Mathews or the Braves included in the magazine.

113. In his four-year high school career playing for Bridgeport High in Ohio, Phil Niekro posted a 17-1 record with his only loss a 1-0 decision as a result of a home run. Which player delivered the decisive blow?

Answer: The only run in the contest came from a four-bagger hit by Bill Mazeroski, who played for Warren Consolidated High School in Tiltonsville in 1954. He would sign a contract with the Pittsburgh Pirates a few weeks later.

114. What Milwaukee Braves player stroked the first hit ever surrendered by Sandy Koufax?

Answer: In an All-Star season when Johnny Logan hit thirty-seven doubles, blasted thirteen home runs, and drove in eighty-three runs, he did manage a bloop-single into right field to capture the first hit recorded against Sandy Koufax.

115. Henry Aaron wore a different number than his #44 he would wear the rest of his career. What was the number, and why did he change?

Answer: Henry Aaron made his MLB debut in 1954, wearing number 5 for the Milwaukee Braves. He deemed the number five lousy luck after a broken ankle sidelined him at the end of his rookie season. Starting in 1955, Aaron wore the number 44 for the rest of his career.

116. Major League Baseball held its twenty-third All-Star Game in Milwaukee's three-year-old County Stadium on July 12, 1955. The exciting contest was decided by superb late-inning relief work and a walk-off home run. Who were the heroes?

Answer: Three Braves made important contributions before the hometown crowd. Johnny Logan cracked an RBI single, Hank Aaron had an RBI and a run scored, and Gene Conley pitched a perfect seventh inning, striking out the side. In the twelfth inning, Stan Musial of the Cardinals won it for the NL with a walk-off home run.

117. Who took over for Charlie Grimm forty-six games into the 1956 season and led the team to World Series glory the following year?

Answer: Upon arriving in Milwaukee, Fred Haney skippered the Braves to a near-miss second-place finish in 1956 and a pennant and a World Championship in 1957. The following year he led the Braves to the World Series for the second straight year against the New York Yankees, which they lost in seven games. In his final year with Milwaukee, the team missed winning their third consecutive pennant by one game. Fred Haney compiled a 341-231 record in his four-year stint with Milwaukee.

118. Why during the early years of his career did Milwaukee's public relations director, Don Davidson, begin referring to Aaron as "Hank," not "Henry," as he was known by those close to him?

Answer: Davidson felt that the less formal name "Hank" was a warmer, more all-American name and made him more accessible to the press and the fans.

119. What backstop was an eleven-time All-Star with the Braves?

Answer: Del Crandall was an excellent pitch-caller, eleven-time All-Star, and four-time Gold Glove Award recipient.

120. What Braves player showed up carrying unexpected hurricane-force winds and helped win the 1957 pennant?

Answer: Bob Hazle stormed onto the Milwaukee scene in August 1957 after Bill Bruton's season ended with a knee injury. From August 9 through August 25, Hazle batted .473 with five home runs and nineteen RBIs during fourteen games, a sudden burst of unexpected offense that earned him the nickname "Hurricane." The left-handed swinger batted .403 with seven home runs and twenty-seven runs batted in during forty-one games. Despite having had just 134 at-bats, he finished fourth in the 1957 NL Rookie of the Year voting.

121. The Braves played in back-to-back World Series in 1957 and 1958. Which team did they play in both series?

(Left to Right) Managers Fred Haney and Casey Stengel

Answer: The Braves battled the New York Yankees in both series, capturing the crown in 1957 and losing to the Yanks in 1958.

122. How many players from the 1957 World Series between the Braves and Yankees are in the Hall of Fame?

Answer: Eight. Four Braves players: Warren Spahn, Henry Aaron, Eddie Mathews, and Red Schoedienst, and four members of the Yankees: Mickey Mantle, Yogi Berra, Whitey Ford, and Casey Stengel.

123. In game two of the 1957 World Series, the Braves' win was the first Fall Classic contest won by a non-New York City team since 1948. What team won the last game in the 1948 Series?

Answer: The Cleveland Indians beat the Boston Braves, 4-3, on October 11, 1948, to win the World Series, 4-2. The Braves would not return to the World Series until 1957.

124. What Braves pitcher had three victories in the 1957 World Series and earned the Most Valuable Player trophy?

Answer: Lew Burdette became the first pitcher in thirty-seven years to win three complete games in a series. Pirates' rookie Babe Adams did so in 1909.

125. What two players received the MVP and Cy Young Awards after the 1957 season?

Answer: Hank Aaron and Warren Spahn. The Braves slugger hit forty-four long balls while batting .322 with 198 hits, 132 RBIs, and 118 runs scored. The left-handed hurler had a record of 21-11 with eighteen complete games and four shutouts. He collected 111 strikeouts while pitching in 271 innings and finished with a 2.69 ERA.

126. Best known as a St. Louis Cardinal, this Hall of Famer was only a Brave for three years. But in his first season wearing the tomahawk, he batted .309 and finished third in the MVP voting while helping to lead the Braves to the NL pennant and their only World Series title in Milwaukee.

Answer: Red Schoendienst played nineteen years with the St. Louis Cardinals, but his first two years wearing a Braves uniform were very impactful. Placing third in the 1957 MVP voting, Red was one of the catalysts that propelled the Milwaukee Braves to the pennant in 1957 and their first World Championship since 1914. After another productive pennant-winning season in 1958, Schoendienst was sidelined in 1959 while going through treatment for tuberculosis.

127. Besides winning three games in a World Series, what other record did Lew Burdette match dating back to the 1905 Fall Classic?

Answer: He was the first since Christy Mathewson in 1905 to pitch two shutouts (game five and seven) in a World Series.

128. This outfielder played in Milwaukee for the first five seasons of his eleven-year career. Who was this Braves outfielder who batted .330 in 1958 with twenty-four home runs and seventy-four RBIs?

Answer: Wes Covington had a great second half in 1957 with twenty-one home runs and sixty-five runs batted in over the final ninety-six games. In the World Series, he made two great defensive plays that saved wins for the Series MVP Lew Burdette. In his final year in Milwaukee, he became one of the few players to ever play for four teams in one season, as he saw action for the Braves, Phillies, Athletics, and the White Sox.

129. Who was this player who had one of the best seasons of his career and led the Braves to the 1957 World Championship over the Yankees?

Answer: You could flip a coin as to whether the 1957 or the 1958 campaign was the best year for the Braves superstar Hank Aaron. There are a number of reasons why 1957 would most likely be viewed as his best in his illustrious career spanning over three decades. The Braves slugger hit forty-four long balls while batting .322 with 198 hits, 132 RBIs, and 118 runs scored. Aaron's performance for the 1957 season propelled the Braves into the World Series against the Yankees, and his performance against New York was remarkable. In the Fall Classic, #44 went eleven for twenty-eight at the plate, recording a .393 average. The Milwaukee slugger hit a triple, three home runs coupled with seven RBIs, and had an outstanding .786 slugging percentage.

130. What two Braves sluggers had a combined total of over 850 home runs?

Answer: Eddie Mathews and Hank Aaron combined for 863 home runs in their thirteen years together, the most in baseball history, in helping propel the Milwaukee Braves to two pennants and their only World Series championship. In their twelve seasons, Babe Ruth and Lou Gehrig hit 859 with the New York Yankees.

131. Who was the only professional athlete in sports history to win a World Championship ring in baseball and basketball?

Answer: Gene Conley pitched for the World Series champion Milwaukee Braves in 1957. He carved out a parallel career in professional basketball, playing during baseball's off-season and winning three NBA titles with the Boston Celtics from 1958 to 1961.

132. In 1957, the baseball glove manufacturer Rawlings created the Gold Glove Award to commemorate the best fielding performance at each position. Al Kaline was the first to be honored as a right-fielder. Who was the second ballplayer to win the award?

Answer: Hank Aaron won the award in 1958, 1959, and 1960. Roberto Clemente was Gold Glove Award winner for twelve consecutive seasons from 1961 through 1972 before his tragic death on New Year's Eve that final year.

133. Who was the Milwaukee Braves player and future Hall of Famer who signed his first contract for the modest amount of $250?

Answer: Braves scout Bill Maughn signed the 19-year-old Phil Niekro in July 1958 for a $275 a month salary. His father would not sign the contract until the Braves kicked in a $500 signing bonus. "Knucksie" pitched in his first game in the Majors in 1964.

134. On May 26, 1959, this Pittsburgh hurler pitched what most experts hail as the greatest game ever thrown by a losing pitcher. After twelve perfect innings, how did Harvey Haddix lose his masterpiece in the thirteenth?

Answer: The five-foot-nine Pittsburgh left-hander lost his perfect game when Felix Mantilla led off the thirteenth inning and reached first on an error. After a sacrifice bunt by Mathews and a walk to Aaron, Haddix lost his no-hitter and the game when Joe Adcock blasted a three-run homer. Because of a baserunning blunder by Aaron (not completely circling the bases when he saw Mantilla cross home plate), Commissioner Ford Frick ruled hours later Adcock would only be awarded a double (and subsequently ruling him and Aaron out) giving the Braves a 1-0 victory. Lew Burdette pitched thirteen shutout innings to earn the win.

135. The Braves broke many attendance records in their twelve seasons in Milwaukee. How many seasons did the Braves attract two million people?

Answer: The Milwaukee fans were baseball crazy. The team led the league in attendance each year from 1954 to 1958, and drew over 2,000,000 fans each of their first four seasons. However, in the team's final year in 1965, they drew only 555,000.

136. In 1959, who was the slugger who won more matches and took home more cash than any other contestant on the popular show Home Run Derby?

Answer: Hank Aaron won in six of his seven appearances and won an estimated $13,500 in prize money.

137. Who was the only player for the Braves franchise to win two batting titles in the twentieth century?

Answer: Hank Aaron won his first batting title (.328) in 1956, collecting 200 hits and thirty-four doubles. He stroked 223 hits to earn his second title with a .355 batting average and a .636 slugging percentage in 1959.

138. In 1960, when Henry Aaron was informed that his new manager was considering moving him from right field to second base, Aaron responded, "I'll play second if he'll play third." Who was the manager?

Answer: Charlie Dressen is the only manager of the seven Aaron played for that he said he didn't get along with.

139. Del Crandall caught three no-hitters in his career with the Milwaukee Braves. All three gems were hurled against the same team. Who was his batterymate for each game, and who was the unfortunate losing team?

Answer: Crandall caught his first no-hitter in 1954 with Jim Wilson on the mound for the Braves. His stellar performance was followed six years later (1960) by no-hit gems by Lew Burdette and Warren Spahn. All three no-nos were thrown against the Philadelphia Phillies.

140. On June 8, 1961, the Milwaukee Braves became the first Major League Baseball team to hit four consecutive home runs in the same inning. Who were the four Braves players that accomplished the rare feat?

Answer: Hank Aaron, Eddie Matthews, Joe Adcock, and Frank Thomas. Slugger Joe Torre came up, following Thomas, with the opportunity to make it five in a row but grounded out.

141. Who was the oldest Brave ever to throw a no-hitter?

Answer: In 1961 against the San Francisco Giants at County Stadium, Warren Spahn threw his second no-hitter at age forty years and five days. Spahnie faced the minimum of twenty-seven batters in a 1-0 shutout, walking Chuck Hiller in the fourth inning.

142. Hank Aaron stole home for the first time when he was involved in a baseball rarity, the triple steal. Which other two players participated in the grand theft?

Answer: Joe Adcock and Joe Torre, recognized more for their power than their speed on the basepaths, startled the Cincinnati Reds with a triple steal in the sixth inning on July 18, 1961.

143. Who was the first Braves pitcher to win 349 games in their uniform?

Answer: Warren Spahn won 349 games and lost 227 in his twenty-two seasons with the Braves. His Hall of Fame career was highlighted by fifteen all-star appearances, two no-hitters, and a Cy Young award. Spahn led the National League in wins eight times and came in second in the Cy Young voting on three occasions. If he hadn't served our country in the military for three years during the prime of his career, some feel Spahny would have ended up with close to 450 career wins.

144. This Brave broke into Major League Baseball as a catcher in 1962 as a Milwaukee Brave. Although he caught in Milwaukee in '62-3, in St. Louis in '64-5, in Philadelphia in '66-7, finishing in Atlanta in 1967, you may know him best by his voice. Who is the current voice of Milwaukee?

Answer: Bob Uecker was one of Phil Niekro's favorite catchers. The weak-hitting backstop once replied when asked how it was catching Phil Niekro, "The way to catch a knuckleball is to wait until it stops rolling and then pick it up." Bob Uecker was inducted in the MLB Hall of Fame for his forty-three years in the announcer's booth for the Milwaukee Brewers.

145. Robin Roberts had excellent control on the mound. His career average of 1.73 walks per nine innings placed him first among modern-day starters with at least 3,000 innings in MLB. He was followed by Greg Maddux (1.80), Carl Hubbell (1.82), and Juan Marichal (1.82). Can you name the fifth leading pitcher with at least 3,000 innings who played after 1920?

Answer: Milwaukee hurler Lew Burdette had a career average of 1.84 walks per nine innings, placing him fifth among modern-day starters with at least 3,000 innings in MLB.

146. Thirty stolen bases and thirty home runs in a season qualify you for the 30/30 Club. Willie Mays (1956 and 1957) and Ken Williams (1922) were the first two players to accomplish this rare feat. Can you name the third?

Answer: Hank Aaron stole 30-plus bases in a single season only once in his career. It occurred in the 1963 campaign. He swiped his thirtieth of the year on September 25, 1963. He'd already hit 40-plus home runs, making him only the third player in Major League history to join the 30/30 Club.

147. Many baseball pundits feel the game featuring Warren Spahn and Juan Marichal on the mound on July 2, 1963, was one of the greatest pitching duels of all time in Major League Baseball. Scoreless after fifteen innings, who won and how?

Answer: At age forty-two, Spahn and twenty-five-year-old Juan Marichal matched up in a pitching duel in 1963 that featured going into the contest Marichal with twelve wins in fifteen decisions for his team and Spahn sporting an 11-3 record. In the thirteenth inning, with the score still scoreless, manager Alvin Dark asked Marichal if he had had enough.  Marichal barked back, "a forty-two-year-old man is still pitching, I can't come out." Spahn lost his bid for his twelfth win of the season when Willie Mays drove a home run through the teeth of the Candlestick Park wind for the game-winner, 1-0. Spahn ended the season leading the National League with twenty-two complete games.

148. In 1963, Hank Aaron led the National League in home runs and RBIs but fell short of winning the Triple Crown. How close did he come to capturing one of baseball's hardest awards to obtain?

Answer: He barely missed winning the Triple Crown, losing the batting title to Tommy Davis by a scant .007 points.

149. Who was the youngest player to hit a home run for the Braves?

Answer: On October 4, 1964, at eighteen years and 329 days of age, Billy Southworth hit his one and only Major League home run while playing for the Milwaukee Braves. Southworth played in just three career Major League games, all with the Braves. His home run came in his final career game. He homered off Pittsburgh's Earl Francis in the third inning. Not only was that his first and only career home run, but it was also one of just two career hits.

150. What Braves pitcher had thirteen seasons with twenty or more wins?

Answer: Warren Spahn is the winningest southpaw pitcher in MLB history., Spahn was victorious in 363 games and won twenty games in a record thirteen seasons, including his last as a forty-year-old.

151. What Braves player who began his career in Milwaukee in 1964 was nicknamed Knucksie?

Answer: Phil Niekro was nicknamed "Knucksie" because of his career success with his challenging-to-hit and sometimes hard-to-control knuckleball. He is perhaps the most outstanding practitioner of the knuckleball. Another prominent knuckleballer, Tom Candiotti, was Niekro's teammate on the Indians in 1986 and said that talking to "Knucksie" about pitching was "like talking to Thomas Edison about light bulbs."

152. Which Braves Hall of Famer, who after hitting thirty or more home runs for nine straight seasons, was the heir apparent to breaking Babe Ruth's record?

Answer: At the age of thirty, Eddie Mathews had already clouted 422 home runs. The left-handed slugger had hit thirty or more home runs for nine straight seasons before his twenty-ninth birthday.

153. What Braves 300-game winner captured the same number of hits at the plate as he did wins on the mound?

Answer: Warren Spahn is credited with 356 victories and 356 base hits in his twenty-year career. In the 1965 season, he would get an additional seven hits and seven wins with the Mets and the Giants.

154. Who was the only player in a Milwaukee Braves uniform during his entire tenure in the city?

Answer: Eddie Mathews played all thirteen years for the Braves while in Milwaukee. Besides playing for the Boston, Milwaukee, and Atlanta Braves, Mathews also played for the Houston Astros and Detroit Tigers.

155. Who was the first Braves player to have his jersey retired and when?

Answer: Considered one of the greatest left-handed pitchers in baseball history, Warren Spahn was the first player in Braves franchise history to have his number retired. His number 21 jersey was retired on December 11, 1965.

156. Who was the only player after 1914 to win twenty-four or more games for the Braves franchise until John Smoltz did so in 1996?

Answer: Tony Cloninger posted a 24-11 record in 1965. He hurled sixteen complete games in the thirty-eight games he started. It was the only time in his twelve-year career he won twenty games. In 19696 John Smoltz posted a 24-8 record, earning him the Cy Young Award.

157. How many former members of the Milwaukee Braves were inducted into Baseball's Hall of Fame as players?

Answer: Five. Eddie Mathews, Warren Spahn, Hank Aaron, Red Schoendienst, and Enos Slaughter played for Milwaukee. Joe Torre also played for the Braves but was inducted into the HOF as a manager.

****

(Mathews and Aaron) Last walk up tunnel at County Stadium

1966-2021

150 Years of Braves Trivia
Atlanta

158. Who tossed out the first ceremonial first pitch in the Braves' first game in Atlanta?

(Left to Right) Mayor Ivan Allen Jr., Governor Carl Sanders

Answer: Mayor Ivan Allen Jr. felt that to be considered a Major League city, Atlanta needed a Major League team. The enthusiasm for sports shared by Atlanta's citizens and business leaders prompted the building of the Atlanta-Fulton County Stadium. After wooing the Braves baseball team from Milwaukee, Wisconsin, Allen was given the honor of throwing out the first pitch at the inaugural game on April 12, 1966. An overflow crowd of 50,671 excited fans was in attendance for opening night against the Pittsburgh Pirates.

159. What Braves stadium was nicknamed "the launching pad." What was its name and the conditions that helped give its name?

Answer: The high elevation and the Southern summer heat made it favorable to home run hitters, resulting in the nickname "The Launching Pad." Atlanta-Fulton County Stadium boasted the highest elevation (over 1,000 feet above sea level), and more home runs were hit per year in this stadium than any other in MLB.
 It retained this distinction for twenty-seven seasons, until the expansion Colorado Rockies team, boasting a mile-high, 5,280 feet, entered the National League in 1993.

160. What Atlanta hurler threw out the first pitch ever for the Atlanta Braves and had a heartbreaking loss on opening night?

Answer: Tony Cloninger threw out the first pitch at 8:12 p.m. on April 12 1966, and performed brilliantly through thirteen innings before taking the loss to Willie Stargell and the Pittsburgh Pirates, 3-2.

161. What Braves player hit the first home run ever in Atlanta-Fulton County Stadium?

Answer: On April 12, 1966, Joe Torre hit the first Major League home run in the history of Atlanta Stadium.

162. What future Atlanta Brave was one of the three brothers who played together in the outfield in an MLB game?

Answer: On September 15, 1963, Felipe Alou joined his brothers Jesus and Matty to become the first and only all-brother outfield to play in an MLB game.

163. What Braves player became the fifth player in MLB history to hit four grand slams before his twenty-third birthday?

Answer: Eddie Mathews hit eight grand slams in his Major League career and four of those came before turning twenty-three.

164. What Braves Pitcher hit two Grand Slam home runs in one game?

Answer: Tony Cloninger hit two grand-slam home runs and a double driving in nine runs on July 3, 1966, against the Giants at Candlestick Park.

165. What Braves player hit leadoff home runs in back-to-back days against Sandy Koufax and Don Drysdale in 1966?

Answer: Felipe Alou is the only Major Leaguer ever to hit lead-off home runs in two successive games twice. He did it on July 26-27 at Houston for the Milwaukee Braves and duplicated the feat on August 9-10, 1966. He opened back-to-back games off Sandy Koufax and Don Drysdale of the Dodgers at Atlanta Stadium. Incidentally, Koufax's record for the '66 season was 27-9 and Drysdale's was 23-12.

166. Who was the first Braves mascot?

Answer: The most popular and recognizable mascot that the Atlanta Braves had is Chief Noc-A-Homa. He was the original mascot of the Milwaukee Braves, and when the team moved to Atlanta, he moved with them. His name is a play on words meaning "Knock a Homer."

167. What Braves pitcher ranks third for all-time home runs hit by a pitcher in the MLB?

Answer: Warren Spahn places third with thirty-five homers. He follows Wes Ferrell (thirty-eight) and Bob Lemon (thirty-seven) in the home run hit parade.

168. The Braves accomplished a feat in Milwaukee that has never been matched by another city of a franchise in Major League Baseball history. What was it?

Answer: They played in Milwaukee for thirteen years without having a losing record.

169. This Cooperstown resident played the first nine seasons of an eighteen-year career with the Milwaukee/Atlanta Braves, primarily as a catcher?

Answer: Joe Torre was a nine-time MLB All-Star; however, he entered the Hall of Fame as one of the most successful baseball managers for twenty-nine years with five different clubs. Torre led the New York Yankees to four World Championships.

170. What former ballplayer with the Braves took over play-by-play duties when the team moved to Atlanta from Milwaukee in 1966?

Answer: Ernie Johnson's fifty-two-year association with the Braves was the longest of anyone in the organization. The 195-pound right-hander was signed by the Boston Braves as an amateur free agent before the 1942 season. Ernie Johnson began his broadcasting career in Milwaukee with the Braves in 1962 and followed the team in their move to Atlanta. Johnson's love affair with Southern listeners lasted until 1999 when he left the broadcast booth. While going through the many passages from the online tributes Braves fans had posted about his father, Ernie Jr. read one that buckled his knees. It said, "When you heard Ernie Johnson do a game, it was like summertime would never end."

171. What future Hall of Fame pitcher that the Braves selected as the twentieth pick in the secondary January draft had his contract voided over a technicality by Baseball's commissioner William Eckert?

Answer: Tom Seaver was drafted by the Braves on January 29, 1966, in the secondary phase of the 1966 Major League Baseball draft, but the pick was voided. They had agreed on a bonus on February 24, 1966, as Seaver signed for a $40,000 contract. However, Baseball Commissioner Eckert ruled that the Braves' deal with Seaver was void because he signed before he had finished his junior season at the University of Southern California.

172. What Braves' All-Star and National League batting champion always played with his wallet in his back pocket?

Answer: Rico Carty didn't trust banks and didn't feel comfortable using the clubhouse valuables box. The lump you would see in his uniform back pocket during games was his wallet.

173. Who hit the first inside-the-park home run for the Atlanta Braves?

Answer: On May 29, 1966, Eddie Mathews hit the first inside-the-park home run in Atlanta Braves franchise history against the Chicago Cubs at Wrigley Field. The aging Braves slugger drove the ball into the thick ivy covering the right-field wall in fabled Wrigley Field. Mathews headed to third with the ball buried in the ivy and the right fielder frantically ripping the green vines from the wall. When the ball finally dropped at the fielder's feet, the third-base coach sent a winded Mathews home. Beating the long throw by a half step, he slid in safely.

174. Who was the first Brave to play in every game in a 162 game season?

Answer: Felix Milan was the first for the Atlanta Braves to compete in all the games on the 1969 schedule. The Puerto Rican native was chosen for the All-Star team and earned the Gold Glove award.

175. What Brave hit the second inside-the-park home run for the franchise after they moved to Atlanta?

Answer: In 1967, Hank Aaron circled the bases for an inside-the-park home run in Philadelphia. It was the only one of his 755 career homers that did not clear the fence. It was the second inside-the-parker since the Braves moved to Atlanta. Eddie Mathews hit the first on May 29, 1966.

176. Satchel Paige reached out to the twenty MLB teams about the prospect of joining them in 1968. The sixty-two-year-old pitcher needed only 158 days on an active roster to reach the five-year minimum required to receive his pension. Nineteen of the organizations turned him down. What owner stood up for the first Negro player to be inducted in the Baseball Hall of Fame?

Answer: The Atlanta Braves owner, Bill Bartholomay, took a different stance and signed the seventeen-year Negro Leagues' veteran premier player. Bartholomay put him on the roster as a pitching coach and advisor. "Satchel Paige is one of the greatest pitchers of all time," Bartholomay told United Press International. "Baseball would be guilty of negligence should it not assure this legendary figure a place in the pension plan."

177. When the Braves won their division in 1969, who was the only twenty-game winner on the staff for the season?

Answer: The Braves finished the season three games in front of the Giants and were led by pitcher Phil Niekro, the only twenty-game winner on the staff. Niekro finished with a 23-13 record in forty starts with 193 strikeouts in 284.1 innings. He was one of the league leaders with a terrific 2.45 ERA. The 1969 pennant would belong to the Mets, who swept the Braves, 3-0. Niekro lost game one by a score of 9-5, giving up nine hits, nine runs (only four earned) with the deciding factor being a five-run eighth inning by the Mets.

178. Who performed in the first concert held at Atlanta Stadium in the summer of 1965?

Answer: When the Beatles played in Atlanta Stadium on Aug. 18, 1965, the concert inaugurated the city's brand-new stadium. Beatlemania was in full swing and 30,000 screaming fans attended the epic event. The twelve–song set began with the crowd-pleasing song "Twist and Shout."

179. Willie Mays is only one of two players to homer with a teammate at least fifty times in the same game with two different teammates. Who was the Braves player who accomplished this rare feat?

Answer: Eddie Mathews did this with Henry Aaron seventy-five times and with Joe Adcock fifty-six times. Willie Mays homered with Willie McCovey sixty-eight times and Orlando Cepeda fifty times in the same games.

180. A famous saying this single-most famous player in the Negro Leagues favored was, "If you didn't know how old you were, how old would you be?" Who was this baseball legend who was the oldest player to pitch in MLB?

Answer: Satchel Paige became the oldest player in Big League history at age fifty-nine when he pitched three innings for the Kansas City A's on September 25, 1965. After joining Atlanta as a coach and advisor, the ageless wonder did pitch an inning against the Braves starting lineup in spring training. He gave up a hit, got Hank Aaron to pop out, and struck out the last two batters he would ever face in Major League Baseball

181. This third baseman for the Braves was part of a brother act that both played third base and won the Gold Glove for that position. Who were these slick-fielding siblings?

Answer: Both Ken and Clete Boyer were Gold Glove recipients. Clete Boyer received the award in 1969 and brother Ken won on five occasions (1958, 1959, 1960, 1961, and 1963). A third brother, Clyod, played in the Majors along with his brothers as a pitcher for St, Louis and Kansas City and was Bobby Cox's pitching coach with the Braves in 1980.

182. He had six hits in a single game on July 6, 1970. Who is this Braves player?

Answer: Second baseman Felix Millan, nicknamed "The Kitten," stroked six hits on July 6, 1970.

183. Nicknamed "Beeg Boy," this Brave won the National League batting title in 1970 with an average of .366. Who was this player that shared the outfield with Hank Aaron in the 1970 All-Star Game?

Answer: Rico Carty was a Brave from 1963 to 1972 and was one of the earliest Dominicans to play Major League Baseball. In his first full season, he finished second to Roberto Clemente in the National League batting championship with a .330 average, finishing the season as runner-up to Dick Allen in the 1964 National League Rookie of the Year ballot. His best season was in 1970. He won the batting title with a .366 average, the highest average since Ted Williams recorded a .388 B.A. in 1957. The Braves left-fielder compiled a thirty-one-game hitting streak in 1970.

184. What Braves player was nicknamed "the roadrunner?"

Answer: Ralph Garr was nicknamed "the roadrunner" because of his speed and cleverness on the base paths. He became so popular with fans in Atlanta that the Braves negotiated exclusive Big-League baseball rights with Warner Bros. Cartoons to use animated scenes of the Looney Tunes character Road Runner on the scoreboard, while the calliope erected behind right field went "beep-beep" like the cartoon character every time Garr reached first base. Garr set the Braves single-season record with 180 singles in 1971.

185. In 1973 three Brave players became the first trio to hit forty or more home runs in the same season. Who were these three sluggers?

Answer: Second baseman Davey Johnson (43), right fielder Hank Aaron (40), and third baseman Darrell Evans (41).

186. What Braves reliever caught Hank Aaron's 715th home run when it flew into the bullpen?

Answer: Tom House, a young reliever for the Braves, caught home run 715 as it cleared the left field fence. He passed up a huge payday by giving the ball to Aaron.

187. What Braves promotion for the fans turned into a real fiasco with the umpires?

Answer: The Braves special promotion, "Frisbee Night," was held on June 29, 1974, in a doubleheader played against the Cincinnati Reds. Fans spent the entire evening littering the field with the Frisbees mostly aimed at left-fielder Pete Rose. The Braves lost the first game of the twin bill, and Brave All-Star Buzz Capra won his ninth straight game of the season, shutting out the Reds and striking out seven in ten innings.

188. In the year Hank Aaron broke Babe Ruth's record, who was the hottest pitcher in MLB in the first half of the 1974 season?

Answer: Buzz Capra was the surprise of the Majors in 1974. The relatively unknown hurler won nine straight games before the All-Star break. While the Braves averaged some 9,000 fans per game for the season, Capra drew 30,000-plus during the streak. He finished the year at 16-8 with eleven complete games and a league-leading 2.33 ERA.

189. Why were the Atlanta Braves nicknamed "America' Team"?

Answer: The Atlanta Braves purported to the name due to their games being broadcast on cable TV systems nationwide on TBS from 1977 to 2007, building a fan base in areas of the United States far removed from a Major League Baseball team.

190. Who was Major League Baseball's first African-American general manager?

Answer: William (Bill) DeVaughn Lucas was the first African-American general manager in Major League Baseball as front-office boss of the Atlanta Braves from mid-September 1976 until his death in early May 1979.

A member of the organization for twenty-three years, he was inducted into the Braves Hall of Fame in 2006. Dale Murphy, who was brought into the Braves organization by Lucas, shared his thoughts about the GM and his friend at the memorial service. "Bill's dream was for this organization to be a success. It is our sacred honor to be chosen to fulfill his dream."

191. What Braves superstar won the MVP and finished in the top three voting for the award on six other occasions?

Answer: Henry Aaron was one of the best to play the game. A complete ballplayer, he possessed speed, power at the plate, and tremendous defensive skills.

192. What Atlanta slugger started straight out of college, refusing to play in the minors, and took home the Rookie of the Year Award?

Answer: Bob Horner hit a home run in his first Major League at-bat against Hall of Famer Bert Blyleven. For the season, in only eighty-nine games, Horner connected for twenty-three home runs, stroked seventeen doubles, had sixty-three RBIs, and took home the Rookie of the Year Award.

193. What Braves reliever shut down Pete Rose's forty-four game hitting streak on August 1, 1978?

Answer: With reliever Gene Garber in the game, Rose lined out (into a double play) to the third baseman in the seventh inning. In the ninth inning, with 45,000 fans screaming at the top of their lungs, Rose faced Garber a second time and struck out (foul-tip into the mitt of catcher Joe Nolan, to end the contest and his forty-four-game streak. The following day a disturbed Rose commented on being shut down by Garber. "He pitched like it was the seventh game of the World Series," complained Rose, who didn't like the fact that Garber nibbled at the plate rather than challenging him. "I don't know what it's like to pitch in the seventh game of the World Series," responded Garber. "He gets paid to get hits, and I get paid to get outs."

194. This pitcher took the mound for the Braves for twenty of his twenty-four seasons. Who was this knuckleball pitcher who twice won and lost twenty games in the same season twice?

Answer: In 1974 Phil Niekro led the league in wins, complete games, and innings pitched, finishing third in the Cy Young voting. He again led the league in wins in 1979 at the age of forty, finishing with the second twenty-win and twenty-loss season of his career.

195. Who was Phil Niekro's batterymate for his 200th win?

Answer: On May 1, 1979, Dale Murphy was the catcher in Phil Niekro's 200th win. For the season, Niekro would post a 21-20 record. Murphy would catch twenty-seven games and play first base for seventy-six that season. The next year he moved to the outfield on a permanent basis, primarily at the center-field position.

196. What two Hall of Fame ballplayers that wore a Braves uniform finished one and two as the all-time RBI leaders in Major League Baseball?

Answer: Hank Aaron broke an RBI record that stood for forty-four years. His RBI total for his twenty-five-year career was 2,297. Hammerin' Hank's most productive season was 1957, a year in which he drove in 132 runs and was awarded the National League's MVP award. Babe Ruth donned a Boston Braves uniform in his final year in Major League baseball. In his last game played on May 25, 1935, the Sultan of Swat belted three home runs and had five RBIs, giving him a career total of 2,214, second behind Aaron.

197. This twenty-three-year Major League veteran holds the record for being selected for the most All-Star games. Can you name this Hall of Famer, and how many of the Summer Classics he attended?

Answer: Hank Aaron was chosen to play in twenty-five MLB All-Star games. The Mid-Summer Classic is usually played the second or third week in July. Two All-Star games were held each season from 1959 to 1962.

198. This player came into the organization as a catcher and then was moved to the first-base position. Who was this fan favorite who became a seven-time All-Star playing centerfield for the Braves?

Answer: In his fifth year in the Majors, Dale Murphy moved to the centerfield position. He captured five Gold Gloves and was MVP in the National League in 1982 and 1983. He was a fan favorite in Atlanta for fifteen years.

199. Which Brave pitcher holds the record for wild pitches thrown in one nine-inning contest?

Answer: Knuckleballer Phil Niekro threw six wild pitches on August 4, 1979. Four of those wild pitches were thrown in the one inning. When former Brave player, Bob Uecker, Niekro's favorite backstop, was asked the best way to catch Niekro's knuckleball, he replied, "The way to catch a knuckleball is to wait until it stops rolling and then pick it up."

200. Hank Aaron is best known for setting the record for most home runs in a career (755), surpassing the previous mark of 714 by Babe Ruth. Many people ask, "What was the longest home run Hank Aaron ever hit?"

Answer: Hank Aaron hit what most consider to be the longest home run of his career on June 18, 1962. He launched a 470-foot moonshot to straight away center field at the Polo Grounds in New York. Only three other players ever hit a ball there—Joe Adcock in 1953 and Lou Brock, who did it the day before Aaron. The fourth player to reach the center-field promise land was Luke Easter in a Negro Leagues game.

201. What Braves Hall of Fame pitcher was named the Major League Baseball's Roberto Clemente Award recipient in 1980?

Answer: Phil Niekro and his wife, Nancy, had served the Atlanta community for over fifty years by taking part in dozens of charitable causes. Major League Baseball awarded him the prestigious Roberto Clemente Award in 1980. Some of the charities he supported through the years include "Batter up for AVM," fighting the battle against brain aneurysm, and a twenty-five-year partnership with Edmondson Telford in Gainesville, Georgia, to fight child abuse. After his death in December, 2021, the Atlanta Braves Foundation presented a $35,000 check to the Edmondson Telford Child Advocacy Center to continue the legacy of his work.

202. Who was the Brave speedster from Monroe, Louisiana, who batted .585 for Grambling State University and joined Atlanta in 1968?

Answer: After retiring from the Major Leagues, Ralph Garr was inducted into the College Baseball Hall of Fame in 2013. He played for the Braves between 1968 and 1975 and was inducted into the Braves Hall of Fame in 2006.

203. What Braves player holds the team record for most doubles?

Answer: Besides holding the Braves franchise record for most home runs hit as a Brave (733) and most base hits (3600), Henry Aaron hit 600 two-baggers.

204. Who is the six-foot-ten Hall of Fame southpaw fireballer who was drafted by the Braves organization but got away?

Answer: Randy Johnson was drafted directly out of high school in 1982 by the Braves in the fourth round and offered $50,000 to sign. Instead, Johnson accepted a full athletic scholarship to play baseball for the University of Southern California. Johnson played for twenty Major League seasons, primarily for Seattle and Arizona. Nicknamed the "Big Unit," his career was highlighted with 303 wins, five Cy Young awards, ten All-Star selections, a winner of the Triple Crown in 2002, and a record-setting 4,775 career strikeouts. He was inducted into the Hall of Fame in 2015. If the Braves could have signed Johnson, it makes you wonder what could have been?

205. "Trying to hit Phil Niekro is like trying to eat jello with chopsticks. Sometimes you get a piece, but most of the time you get hungry." Who said this?

Answer: Bobby Murcer of the New York Yankees is credited with making the amusing remark on the difficulty of hitting Niekro's knuckleball.

206. What is the longest winning streak for a Braves team to begin a season?

Answer: In 1982, the Braves jumped out to an amazing 13-0 start and finished the season with an 89-73 mark. Although they broke out at the beginning of the season, they failed to win the National League pennant, as they lost to the Cardinals in the NLCS.

207. Our fan club bought ninety of them for Braves opening night. How much was a dugout-level ticket in 1983?

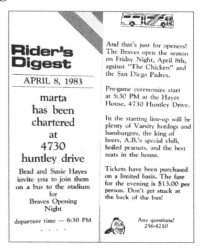

Answer: An Atlanta-Fulton County Stadium dugout level ticket in 1983 cost you $7.50. In 2018, dugout seats above either dugout in Suntrust Park ran you between $114-$141 a ticket.

208. Ninety pitchers have struck out four batters in an inning in MLB, which occurs when a catcher drops the ball on a third strike and the batter advances to first. What Brave pitcher joins two other members of the 3,000-Strikeout Club to accomplish this feat?

Answer: Braves' knuckleballer Phil Niekro joined Bob Gibson and Walter Johnson to strike out 3,000 batters in their career and whiff four batters in an inning.

209. Which Brave was the Most Valuable Player of the National League in back-to-back years?

Answer: Dale Murphy won the Most Valuable Player Award in both 1982 and 1983. In 1982 Murphy played in all 162 scheduled games.

210. What Braves pitcher from the Dominican Republic missed his scheduled start when he got lost on his way to the stadium and spent several hours circling around the I-285 perimeter three times?

Answer: Pascual Perez was slotted in the lineup to pitch for the Braves on August 19, 1982. Having recently received his driver's license, he chose to drive to the stadium for the first time, got lost, and found himself circling the perimeter over and over. He arrived three hours late and ten minutes after the game had started. Perez's driving error lightened the mood for the Braves, who were reeling from a slump that saw them lose nineteen of twenty-one games. Phil Niekro took Perez's place on the mound and pitched the team to victory.

211. What Braves player received the highest percentage of votes for his admission into the MLB Hall of Fame?

Answer: Henry Aaron received one of the highest percentage votes ever for a Brave, receiving 97.8 percent of the vote in 1982. Not far behind was Greg Maddux's percentage of votes tallied at 97.2 in the year 2014.

212. Can you name five fan appreciation events Ted Turner and his public relations director, Bob Hope, put on in the seventies and eighties to increase attendance at the ballpark?

Answer: The Ostrich Race, The Scramble for Cash, Wrestling Night in the Bullpen, Wedding Night in the Stadium, and The Great Wallenda's Walk. Frisbee Night and The Peanut Push with Ted Turner were others.

213. What Braves ballplayer walked five times in a single game on two occasions?

Answer: Dale Murphy drew five walks on April 22, 1983, and was given a free pass five times again on May 23, 1987.

214. What Braves second baseman, with his brother Hank, holds the record for all-time home runs for a brothers' duo in Major League Baseball?

Answer: The Aaron brothers, Tommy and Hank hold the MLB record with a combined 768 home runs. Tommy had 13, and Hank had 755. At a distant second, the Murray brothers, Rick (4) and Eddie Murray (504) launched a combined 508 four-baggers.

215. What Atlanta Braves Hall of Famer was drafted by both the National Hockey League and Major League Baseball?

Answer: In 1984 Tom Glavine was drafted by the National Hockey League's Los Angeles Kings, as well as the Braves.

216. The name for the Rookie of the Year was changed in July of 1987. Why was this appropriate?

Answer: Jackie Robinson, the Brooklyn Dodgers' second baseman, won the inaugural award in 1947. It was renamed the Jackie Robinson Award in his honor and for his contributions to the game. Alvin Dark of the Milwaukee Braves was the recipient of the second Rookie of the Year Award in 1948.

217. This Braves ballplayer who wore both a Milwaukee and Atlanta uniform was the most frequent guest in the history of the Johnny Carson show? Who was the man many referred to as "Mr. Baseball?"

Answer: Known for his humor, beer commercials, and his jokes about his undistinguished playing career, Bob Uecker actually became much better known after he retired from playing. A wonderful and amusing conversationalist, he made some 100 guest appearances on Johnny Carson's *The Tonight Show*. His gift for gab has been instrumental in his successful forty years in the booth for the Milwaukee Brewers. He was honored by the National Baseball Hall of Fame with its 2003 Ford C. Frick Award in recognition of his broadcasting career.

218. Having only hit five home runs and eight triples in his nine-year career, what Brave hit for the cycle (single, double, triple, and home run in the same game) on September 23, 1987, against Houston?

Answer: Albert Hall had his best season for the Braves in 1987, appearing in ninety-two games and batting a career-best .284. He became the first Brave to steal thirty or more bases in less than a hundred games when he swiped thirty-three bases, and the first Brave to hit for the cycle since John Bates in 1907 and Duff Cooley to achieve this feat many feel is more difficult and rarer than pitching a no-hitter. Ironically, hitting for the cycle was nothing new for Hall. He also did it in 1982 while playing for Triple-A Richmond.

219. What decade in the twentieth century did the Braves franchise not have a twenty game-winner?

Answer: Atlanta did not have a pitcher on its staff that won twenty games in the 1980s. Knuckleballer Phil Niekro won seventeen games twice in that decade. In the 1979 season, Niekro won twenty-one contests at the age of forty.

220. John Smoltz had an illustrious pitching career with the Braves, spanning twenty-one years. Which team originally picked Smoltzie in the 1985 amateur draft?

Answer: The Detroit Tigers chose John Smoltz as the 574th overall pick in the twenty-second round of the 1985 Amateur draft. In 1987, the twenty-one-year-old right-hander was traded to the Braves for pitcher Doyle Alexander. At the time the young Smoltz was disappointed and heartbroken from being traded from his hometown.

221. What Braves pitcher, with his brother Joe, holds the record for all-time wins for a brothers' duo in Major League Baseball?

Answer: The Niekro brothers, Phil and Joe hold the MLB record with a combined 539 wins. Phil had 318 wins, and Joe had 221. Not far behind, Gaylord and Jim Perry won a combined 529 wins. The Niekro brothers faced each other nine times, with Joe winning five of the contests and Phil winning four.

222. Who was the third slugger in Braves franchise history to clout four four-baggers in a single contest?

Answer: Bob Horner connected for four home runs on July 6, 1986. Horner hit solo home runs in the second and fourth innings and smacked a three-run four-bagger in the fifth. He finished his remarkable day with another solo homer in the ninth.

223. What Braves Hall of Fame pitcher's first full season resulted in a 7-17 record?

Answer: Tom Glavine had nine starts in 1987 and had a 2-4 record. In his first full Major League season, he started thirty-four contests and posted a 7-17 record over 195.1 innings. His first twenty-win season was in 1991, helping the Braves capture their first of fourteen in-a-row division titles. Glavine persevered, and his career numbers were 305-203 with a 3.54 ERA and 2,607 strikeouts. He was a ten-time All-Star and earned Cy Young Awards in 1991 and 1998.

224. What Braves pitcher won 121 games after his fortieth birthday between the years 1980 and 1987?

Answer: In a span of seven years after his fortieth birthday, Phil Niekro won 121 games. He earned two Gold Gloves and was picked on two All-Star teams. After a twenty-year career with the Braves in Milwaukee and Atlanta, he played for four other ball clubs before returning to Atlanta for his last season at age forty-eight. Niekro finished his career with a lifetime win-loss record of 318-274 and pitched two no-hitters. Only Cy Young, Pud Galvin, and Walter Johnson have been on the mound for more innings than Niekro's 5,404.

225. What Braves MVP winner in the years 1982 and 1983 was awarded the "Roberto Clemente Award" in 1988?

Answer: The award is given annually to a player who demonstrates the values Hall of Famer Roberto Clemente displayed in his commitment to the community and understanding the value of helping others. Dale Murphy, a four-time nominee, is actively involved in the Cystic Fibrosis Society and serves as a member of the national board of the Huntington's Disease Society, and has been a spokesman for the Georgia March of Dimes, the American Heart Association, the Georgia PTA and the Arthritis Foundation. "I am honored to receive an award of this kind," Murphy said. "That it is in the name of Roberto Clemente means a great deal to me."

226. What Brave has the longest consecutive games played streak in franchise history?

Answer: Dale Murphy played in 740 consecutive games, at the time the eleventh longest such streak in baseball history.

227. What former Brave franchise players and members of the Hall of Fame played with at least seven teams during their Major League careers?

Answer: Dan Brouthers, King Kelly, Deacon White, Gaylord Perry, Al Simmons, and Hoyt Wilhelm.

228. Only two Major League players have hit four home runs in a game their team lost, the first being Ed Delahanty. Who was the second?

Answer: On July 13, 1896, Delahanty became the second player in the Major Leagues to hit four home runs in a game. He was the first to do so in a losing effort. The Phillies lost, 9-8. On July 6, 1986, Bob Horner blasted four home runs in a loss against the Expos.

229. Who were the "Young Guns" on the Atlanta Braves?

Answer: Steve Avery, John Smoltz, Tom Glavine, Tommy Greene and Kevin Millwood.

230. What Braves team was referred to as the "worst to first" ball club?

Answer: The 1991 Braves became the first team in the National League to go from last place one year to first place the next. They met the Minnesota Twins in the World Series and were defeated in seven games.

231. Not even base stealing champion Ricky Henderson accomplished this feat. What Brave shares the modern-day record with two other players for most stolen bases in a single contest?

Answer: On June 16, 1991, Otis Nixon entered the record books with six stolen bases in a single game. That record has since been matched by Eric Young of the Colorado Rockies in 1996 and Carl Crawford of the Tampa Bay Rays in 2009.

232. Who was the only Brave besides Warren Spahn to pitch in two no-hit games?

Answer: On September 11, 1991, starter Kent Merker combined with relievers Mark Wohlers and Alejandro Pena to no-hit the Padres in a 1-0 victory. Merker pitched the first six innings. The second no-hitter was a solo effort by Mercker, as he no-hit the Los Angeles Dodgers on April 8, 1994. This no-hitter is the last to be pitched by a Brave.

233. Ted Turner always enjoyed company. Who were two well-known celebrities that often sat with him in his Braves first-base box?

Answer: Actress and girlfriend Jane Fonda and former President Jimmy Carter.

234. Who beat the Braves in the 1992 World Series?

Answer: The Toronto Blue Jays beat the Braves in one of the most exciting Fall Classics ever played in seven games.

235. Which Braves pitcher was an integral part of a staff nicknamed the "young guns" and earned MVP honors for the 1991 NLCS series pitching 16 ⅔ scoreless innings against the Pirates?

Answer: The 1991 season was a good year for both Steve Avery and the Braves. The team
went from worst to first in the NL West while Avery compiled a record of 18-8. Avery shut out the Pirates from the fifth inning of game seven in one of the greatest finishes in Braves history.

236. Unfortunately, this left-hander is remembered by many as the reliever that gave up the game-winning home run in game seven of the 1991 World Series. Who was this hard-luck loser that, as a starter, was a contributing factor in Atlanta's incredible "worst to first" finish to win the National League pennant in 1991?

Answer: Charlie Leibrandt was a member of one of only two trios in the MLB history of southpaws to win fifteen games on the same staff, sharing that honor with Tom Glavine and Steve Avery.

237. Warren Spahn became the second pitcher in the Majors to be awarded the Cy Young Award, following inaugural recipient Don Newcombe. Who was the next Brave to win this prestigious award?

Answer: Tom Glavine was the second Brave in franchise history to earn the CYA. His stellar 1991 season showcased a 20-11 record with a league-leading nine complete games.

238. What Brave made the most infamous catch in Braves history?

Answer: On a Saturday night in July 1992, Otis Nixon made one of the most unforgettable catches for the Atlanta Braves. The home team held a one-run lead as a result of a David Justice second-inning home run and a four-hit shutout by Braves starter Charlie Leibrandt against the Pittsburgh Pirates. "The catch" saved all that, ending the game and securing the victory for Atlanta.

239. What is regarded as the most famous slide in Braves baseball history?

Answer: The Sid Bream Slide in the 1992 National League Championship Series, beating Barry Bonds' throw and scoring the winning run against his former team, the Pittsburgh Pirates, propelling Atlanta to the World Series.

240. What Braves pinch-hitter drove in two runs with two outs to give his team the victory in game seven of the National League Championship Series?

Answer: Amazingly when called on to pinch-hit in game seven, Francisco Cabrera had batted only ten times during the 1992 season. On a two-strike pitch, Cabrera delivered a line-drive single off Pirates reliever Stan Belinda. David Justice scored first, and the hustling Sid Bream arrived at home plate a split-second before Bobby Bond's throw from left field, sliding under the tag for the winning run before fifty thousand hysterical fans.

241. What Atlanta player was the only professional athlete to dress out for a playoff game in two different sports on the same day in two different cities?

Answer: On April 27, 1992, Deion Sanders graced the cover of *Sports Illustrated* with the headline reading, "Red-hot Deion Sanders is a big hitter in two sports." Five months later Sanders dressed out for games with the Atlanta Falcons and the Atlanta Braves on the same day. He returned two kickoffs, a punt, and caught a pass. His work at defensive back helped defeat the Dolphins. He dressed out for the Braves but did not play in the night game against the Reds.

242. Who was the National League's Most Valuable Player in 1991 and runner-up in 1992?

Answer: Terry Pendleton was the MVP in the 1991 season. He had led the Braves from a last-place finish the year prior to a division title and a pennant. He had his best individual season in 1991, finishing with a .319 batting average and 187 hits, both of which led the National League. He hit a career-high twenty-two home runs and eight triples. In 1992, he played in 160 games, batted .311, smacked twenty-one home runs, and scored ninety-four runs. He had 105 RBIs, which ranked second in the National League and marked the only time he passed 100 RBIs in his career. Also, he collected 199 hits, which led the National League.

243. What player traded to the Braves on July 20, 1993, sparked a fire in the press box and in the team in their comeback run for the title?

Answer: Fred McGriff brought some heat to the lineup just a few hours after being traded to the Braves when he hit a game-tying home run. Ted Turner had said earlier that day: "Today the stadium caught fire, and so too (with Fred McGriff) will the Braves. The Fire Dog (a reference to a fire in the press-box of Atlanta Fulton County Stadium the day the Braves acquired him from the Padres)."

244. What number one draft pick severely tore his ACL in spring training in 1994 after having only three at-bats (1993) in the Major Leagues?

Answer: After just three plate appearances in 1993, Chipper Jones was pegged as a starter for the 1994 season when tragedy struck. He tore his ACL trying to beat out a hit in spring training, causing uncertainty for his future. He would miss the entire 1994 campaign.

245. What pitcher won three straight Cy Young awards for the Braves?

Answer: Braves All-Star Hall of Fame hurler Greg Maddux won four consecutive Cy Young awards, the first with the Cubs (1992) and the next three with the Braves (1993-1995).

246. The Braves have had fourteen no-hitters thrown in their 150-year history. Who threw the last no-no?

Answer: Kent Mercker threw the last no-hitter by a Brave pitcher on April 8, 1994, exactly twenty years to the day after Hank Aaron broke Babe Ruth's home run record.

247. Who is the only Brave member with his number retired by the franchise who isn't a member of the National Baseball Hall of Fame?

Answer: The Braves have retired ten numbers in their franchise history. Dale Murphy's jersey number 3 was retired by Atlanta on June 13, 1994. The two-time National League MVP is the only individual with a Braves retired number who is not in the Hall of Fame at Cooperstown. Murphy never received the seventy-five percent vote needed to send him into the Hall. His future admission now lies in the hands of the Veterans Committee.

248. What two positions did Chipper Jones regularly play for the Braves?

Answer: Jones was drafted out of college as a shortstop but spent his entire career playing left field and primarily third base for the Braves from 1995 to 2012.

249. What Brave accounted for the only run in game six propelling Atlanta to the 1995 World Series Championship?

Answer: On October 28, 1995, with the help of Tom Glavine and Mark Wohlers' one-hit pitching, David Justice gave Atlanta all the offense needed with a 350-foot blast off Cleveland's reliever, Jim Poole.

250. What is Chipper Jones' real first name and what number did he wear for the nineteen seasons he played for Atlanta?

Answer: Larry wore #10.

251. What Brave Hall of Famer became the first Roberto Clemente Award recipient for the franchise in seventeen years?

Answer: John Smoltz accepted the prestigious Roberto Clemente Award before game three of the 1995 World Series. Commissioner Bud Selig and Roberto Clemente Jr. joined Smoltz at the podium to present the award. Smoltz and his wife, Dyan, who joined him for the ceremony, formed the John and Dyan Smoltz Foundation in 1997 to support their many philanthropic endeavors, including the Kings Ridge Christian School in the Atlanta area. Smoltz's earliest community endeavors date back to 1992 when he began associating himself with the Atlanta Food Bank and Children's Healthcare of Atlanta. With the Food Bank, he helped raise money through golf tournaments and silent auctions.

252. Who was awarded the MVP of baseball's 1995 World Series?

Answer: Tom Glavine took home the MVP trophy by pitching the Braves to two victories, the last a magnificent one-hit shutout of the Indians.

David Justice supplied the only offense needed with a home run in the sixth inning.

253. What year did the Braves set the record for the highest attendance in franchise history?

Answer: After two straight World Series appearances, Atlanta drew a record for the franchise 3,884,720 fans in 1993. They ranked second out of fourteen teams in the NL.

254. Prior to game six in the 1995 World Series, what Braves player ripped the fan base for not showing enthusiasm during their postseason run?

Answer: After criticizing the Atlanta fans in the morning paper for not showing the support for the team like they had in the previous World Series, David Justice was booed when he came to bat in the sixth inning. Those jeers turned into cheers after Justice hit a World Series-winning solo home run off Indian pitcher Jim Poole. The boo birds had become David Justice fans once again.

255. Who is this highly regarded two-sport athlete that played in both the World Series and the Super Bowl?

Answer: Many feel that Deion Sanders, nicknamed "Prime Time" and "Neon Deion," was the greatest multi-sport professional athlete that ever lived. In the 1992 World Series, "Prime Time" stroked eight hits in fifteen at-bats and stole five bases. Sanders helped the 49s to a decisive victory in Super Bowl XXIX. In 1995–96 he won another Super Bowl title in his first season with the Dallas Cowboys.

256. What were the two longest balls ever hit in Atlanta-Fulton County Stadium?

Answer: The longest home run hit at the stadium was 475 feet by the Cubs' Willie Smith, June 10, 1969. During the 1996 Summer Olympics, Cuba's Orestes Kindelan hit a ball 521 feet.

257. What was the strongest come-from-behind postseason series wins in Braves franchise history?

Answer: In 1996, the Braves stormed back from a 3-1 deficit in the post-season, a feat that has never been matched. Maybe just as impressive is the manner in which they dominated the Cards in the final three games. Atlanta outscored St. Louis (32-1) to advance to the World Series.

258. What Braves pitcher holds the record for the most consecutive wins?

Answer: The year that brought the Olympic games to Atlanta also added a Cy Young award to John Smoltz's trophy case. The fireballing right-hander won a franchise-record fourteen straight decisions in 1996 from April 9 to June 19 and led the Majors with 276 strikeouts and wins, finishing the season at 24-8.

259. What Brave was the youngest player to ever homer in a World Series game?

Answer: On October 20, 1996, at the age of nineteen, rookie Brave Andruw Jones homered in his first two at-bats in game one of the 1996 World Series against the New York Yankees in their home park.

260. In what season did the Braves capture the most wins in franchise history?

Answer: The 1998 team's 106 wins are the most in franchise history.

261. Who were the four pitchers on Atlanta's 1997 pitching staff that many rate as one of the best rotations in the history of the MLB?

Answer: Denny Neagle (20-5), Tommy Glavine (14-5), Greg Maddux (19-4), and John Smoltz (15-12).

262. In 1997 Atlanta set a record for most grand-slam home runs hit in a season that still stands. Eight players hit twelve four bases-loaded four-baggers. Can you name the three players that hit more than one?

Answer: Chipper Jones (3), Ryan Klesko (2), and Jeff Blauser (2). Javy Lopez, Keith Lockhart, Tim Spehr, Andruw Jones, and Eddie Perez hit one each.

263. How many World Series did Atlanta play in the 1990s?

Answer: Five. 1991 vs. Minnesota Twins, 1992 vs. Toronto Blue Jays, 1995 vs. Cleveland Indians, 1996 vs. New York Yankees, and 1999 vs. New York Yankees.

264. In 1998, Atlanta had four players hit thirty or more home runs. Can you name the four Sluggers?

Answer: Andres Galarraga (44), Javy Lopez (34), Chipper Jones (34), and Andruw Jones (31).

265. Starting in 1999, the MLB began giving out the Warren Spahn Award to the best left-handed pitcher in baseball. Who was the first recipient of the prestigious award?

Answer: Randy Johnson won the award the first four years it was given. His record 1999-2002 was 81-27. Johnson was drafted by the Atlanta Braves directly out of high school in 1982. He was picked in the fourth round and offered $50,000 to sign. Instead, Johnson accepted a full athletic scholarship to play for the University of Southern California.

266. Can you name four Hall of Famers that only played for the Braves franchise for one year?

Answer: Rogers Hornsby (1928), Babe Ruth (1935), Hoyt Wilhelm (1969), and Gaylord Perry (1981).

267. What Braves player was nicknamed "Mad Dog?"

Answer: Greg Maddux had two nicknames: "Mad Dog" and "the Professor."

268. In 1999, the Major League Baseball All-Century Team was chosen by popular vote of fans. The three biggest vote-getters for the original thirty-man squad were Lou Gehrig (1,297,992), Babe Ruth (1,158,044), and Hank Aaron (1,156,782). What other legendary Brave was honored?

(Left to Right) Roger Clemens, Bob Gibson, Sandy Koufax, Nolan Ryan, & Warren Spahn.

Answer: Warren Spahn was one of ten pitchers honored on the Major League Baseball All-Century Team of thirty players. He joined the prestigious company of Roger Clemens, Bob Gibson, Sandy Koufax, and Nolan Ryan.

269. What player was Bobby Cox referring to when he said he was "the best, smartest, and the most competitive pitcher" he ever saw?

Answer: Greg Maddux.

270. What two-time Braves All-Star became the first Dominican Republican to manage a Major League baseball team?

Answer: In 1992 former Braves outfielder/first baseman Felipe Alou made history by becoming the first native of the Dominican Republic to manage a Major League team. Two years after taking over the helm of the Montreal Expos in 1992, the Expos had the best record in the Majors until the mid-August strike that ended up canceling the entire postseason, thereby denying them a chance to get to their first World Series. Alou was named the NL National League Manager of the Year in 1994, compiling a 74-40 record, the Expos finishing six games ahead of the Braves and named the pennant-winner for the season.

271. Can you name the three pitchers that played for the Braves that won every Cy Young Award in the N.L. except one between 1991-1998?

Answer: Greg Maddux won four Cy Young Awards from 1992-1995, three in a row with Atlanta. Tom Glavine earned the award in 1991 (20-11, .255 ERA, 9 complete games), and 1998 (20-6, .247 ERA, and .769 WP). John Smoltz took home the CYA in 1996 after leading the league in wins and innings pitched and posting a 24-8 record. He also set a franchise record with fourteen straight wins.

272. Only two Braves franchise managers have won five pennants in the same decade. Bobby Cox did so in the nineties (1991, 1992, 1995, 1996, 1999). Can you name the other manager that achieved this extraordinary feat for the organization?

Answer: A full century before Bobby Cox, Frank Selee skippered the Boston Beaneaters to five pennants between 1890 and 1899. His teams captured the flag in 1891, 1892, 1893, 1897, and 1898.

273. In the year 2002, this Brave became only the second pitcher in Major **League Baseball history to record both a twenty-win season and a fifty-save season in his career. Who is this Brave Hall of Famer?**

Answer: John Smoltz pitched for twenty-two big league seasons, all but the last one with the Atlanta Braves. He was an eight-time All-Star, 1995 World Series champion, Cy Young Award winner, and 2005 Roberto Clemente Award recipient. He was the win and strikeout leader in the National League on two occasions and led the league with fifty-five saves in 2002. The Braves retired Smoltz's jersey # 27 in 2012.

274. What is a trade the Atlanta Braves made on December 23, 2003, that many deem one of the worst trades made in the franchise's 150-year history?

Answer: The Braves picked Adam Wainwright in the first round of the 2000 draft and traded him to the Cardinals without playing an inning in the Big Leagues for John Drew. J.D. had a thirty-one home run season for the Braves before departing to the Dodgers after one season. Wainwright has pitched for sixteen seasons (184-105) for the Cards, placing in the top three of the CYA voting on four occasions. The thirty-nine-year-old posted a 17-7 record in 2021, leading the league with three complete games.

275. Who was the first Brave to turn in an unassisted triple-play?

Answer: Rafael Furcal achieved one of baseball's rarest feats on August 10, 2003.

276. In 2003 Javier Lopez set the record with forty-three home runs hit during the season while playing the catcher's position. Whose record did he break?

Answer: Todd "Hot Rod" Hundley hit forty-one for the New York Mets in 1996.

277. Who was the first Brave to hit fifty home runs in a single season?

Answer: Braves center fielder Andruw Jones hit fifty-one home runs and drove in 128 runs during the 2005 season. Jones won the Hank Aaron Award and Silver Slugger award for his exceptional performance. Surprisingly the greatest home run hitter of all time, Henry Aaron, never hit fifty in a season.

278. Besides Dennis Eckersley (190 wins, 390 saves), who is the only other player in MLB history to record more than 150 saves and 150 wins in a career?

Answer: In the first twelve years of his career, John Smoltz was employed by the Braves as a starter. Smoltz was converted to a reliever in 2001 after his recovery from Tommy John surgery and spent four years as the team's closer before returning to a starting role. In 2002, he set a National League record with fifty-five saves. His career totals were 213 wins and 154 saves.

279. How many rookies did the Braves have on their roster in 2005?

Answer: Eighteen. This was the biggest number of rookies the Braves ever carried on their ball club in one season, and they still won their division in 2005. The list of Braves' rookie class included such rising-star players as Jeff Francoeur, Kelly Johnson, and Brian McCain.

280. Having played in seventy-three games in 2005, this Braves outfielder finished third in the voting for the Rookie of the Year Award and appeared on the cover of Sports Illustrated as "The Natural." Who was this free-swinging newcomer?

Answer: Jeff Francoeur for the Braves and seven other ball clubs in his twelve-year Major League Baseball career. In his rookie season he immediately showed off his credentials as a five-star baseball player: power at the plate, hitting for a good average, great defensive skills, a rocket arm, and immense popularity with the fans. In less than a half-season in the "Bigs," he had a .315 batting average, slugged fourteen home runs, drove in forty-five runs, and led the league with thirteen assists as an outfielder. When his playing days ended, Francoeur joined the sportscasting corps. Recently he was appointed as a lead television analyst for Braves games.

281. The Braves pitchers have won seven Cy Young Awards since the award was first given. What pitcher for the franchise was the first honored?

Answer: In 1957, Warren Spahn was the Braves' first recipient of the CYA in only the second year it was given. It was originally awarded to the best pitcher in the entire Major Leagues before starting to recognize the best in each league in 1967. Spahn posted an impressive 21-11 record with a 2.69 ERA.

282. Which Braves player captured the first National League Rookie of the Award in the twenty-first century?

Answer: Rafael Furcal swiped forty bases, smacked twenty doubles, and batted .295 to earn the NL ROY award.

283. In the 2005 National League playoff series, game four between the Astros and Braves became the longest game in Major League Baseball's postseason. In what inning was the game decided and who won to advance to the National League championship series?

Answer: Chris Burke's eighteenth inning walk-off home run off Brave rookie reliever Joey Devine punched the Astros ticket to play the St. Louis Cardinals to decide which National League team to advance to the World Series. In addition to being at the time the longest postseason game in MLB history, it was also the only postseason game to include two grand slams, by Lance Berkman and Adam LaRoche. Even more remarkable than the game's length, perhaps, is the fact that the fan who caught Chris Burke's walk-off homer in the eighteenth was the same fan who had caught Lance Berkman's grand slam in the eighth (Section 102, Row 2, Seat 15); the fan later donated both balls to the Baseball Hall of Fame.[12]

284. What Brave won ten straight Gold Glove awards before reaching the age of thirty?

Answer: Center fielder Andruw Jones was awarded ten Gold Glove awards between 1998 and 2007. Jones became the twelfth player in history to hit 300 home runs before his thirtieth birthday.

285. In 2005 Atlanta set an MLB record by having more than five rookies on the team that had at least 100 at-bats. Can you name them?

Answer: Jeff Francoeur (257), Brian McCann (180), Kelly Johnson (290), Roger Langerhans (326), and William Betemit (246).

286. What is the only game in postseason history to feature both teams hitting grand slams?

Answer: Game four of the 2005 National League Division Series, when the Astros and Braves each hit one. The Red Sox became the first team in postseason history to hit two grand slams in one game on the way to a 9-5 win over the Astros. J.D. Martinez hit a grand slam in the first, and then in the second, Rafael Devers.

287. Only three pitchers in the twenty-first century have started more than thirty-five games in a season. Two of these pitched for the Atlanta Braves. Can you name the dynamic duo?

Answer: Tom Glavine in 2002 and Greg Maddux in 2003 (Roy Halladay of Toronto in 2003), each with thirty-six starts.

288. What Atlanta Brave was inducted into the inaugural class of the National College Baseball Hall of Fame in 2006 along with Will Clark, Brooks Kieschnick, Dave Winfield, and Robin Ventura?

Answer: Bob Horner was a college All-American in 1977 and 1978. He set a then-NCAA record of fifty-eight career home runs for Arizona State, set a twenty-five-homer single-season record, and was selected the MVP of the 1977 College World Series. Horner was drafted by Atlanta with the first overall pick in the 1978 amateur draft.

289. What former Atlanta Brave was the starting pitcher in two of the longest games ever played in the postseason in MLB history?

Answer: Tim Hudson got the starting call on August 9, 2005, in an eighteen-inning affair with the Houston Astros, who beat the Braves, 7-6. He started for San Francisco on August 4, 2014, a contest that also was played for eighteen stanzas with the Giants victorious over the Washington Nationals, 2-1.

290. Who was one of the greatest scouts in the history of Major League Baseball and a highly valued member of the Braves' organization for fifty years?

Answer: Paul Synder spent his entire fifty-year professional baseball career in the Braves' organization. Working with then-general managers Bill Lucas and John Mullen, Snyder was a major architect of the Braves' strong early 1980s teams under Manager Joe Torre. When Atlanta went through a prolonged rebuilding process after winning the 1982 NLWD championship, Snyder was scouting director and assisted the general manager in drafting and developing the talent base—players such as Tom Glavine, Steve Avery, David Justice, Jeff Blauser, and Chipper Jones—that served as the foundation for the Braves' string of first-place teams of the 1990s through 2005.

291. It is very rare for an athlete to play in two professional sports during their professional career. Can you name four that did so in the Braves franchise history?

Answer: Jim Thorpe (Boston Braves~1932, Canton Bulldogs~1915-1920), Gene Conley (Boston Braves~1952, Milwaukee Braves~1954-1958, pro basketball~six seasons), Deion Sanders (Atlanta Braves~1991-1994, pro football~fourteen seasons), and Brian Jordan (Atlanta Braves~1999-2001, 2005-2006, pro football~three seasons).

292. In what year did these two Braves' all-time radio announcer favorites leave the booth?

L. to R. Joe Simpson, Don Sutton, Pere van Wieren, and Skip Caray

Answer: In 2008, Braves fans lost two of the greatest announcers to ever serve the franchise in its 150-year history. Skip Caray and Pete Van Wieren were more than announcers. They were your friend telling you a "good night" story about baseball. They connected generations of Brave fans to the team. Also pictured is Don Sutton who served as a broadcaster in Atlanta for twenty-eight years. Don passed away in 2021.

293. What ball player launched only the second walk-off grand slam in MLB history to give the Braves one of their most memorable wins in franchise history?

Answer: It doesn't get more thrilling than this. On May 20, 2010, the Braves entered the ninth inning in a key stretch of the season, trailing by six runs. A never say die rally cut the lead by three when manager Bobby Cox called on Brooks Conrad to pinch-hit with the bases loaded and the Braves trailing, 9-6. He hit a walk-off grand slam against Cincinnati, capping an eight-run comeback for his team.

294. What two Braves came in first and second in the MLB Rookie of the Year voting in 2011?

Answer: Craig Kimbrel became the Braves closer as a rookie in 2011 and set an MLB record for saves with forty-six. He led the National League in saves for four consecutive seasons, from 2011 through 2014. Freddie Freeman finished the 2011 year batting .282 with thirty-two doubles, twenty-one home runs, and seventy-six RBIs in 157 games played.

295. Can You name three Braves that played professionally in Japan after their playing days in MLB were over?

Answer: Johnny Logan (Nankai Hawks~1964), Clete Boyer (Taiyo Whales~1972-1975), and Bob Horner (Yakult Swallows~1987).

296. Since 1915 Greg Maddux for the Braves has posted the third-lowest ERA for a starting pitcher in a season. Can you name the two leaders?

Answer: Bob Gibson (1.12 ERA~1968), Dwight Gooden (1.53 ERA~1985), Greg Maddux (1.56 ERA~1994).

297. Who is the only MLB Hall of Fame member who played with the Braves as the only player to play exclusively for their franchise?

Answer: In the modern era, Braves superstar and Hall of Famer Chipper Jones played for the Braves franchise from 1995 to 2012. Jones was the number one pick in the 1990 MLB draft.

298. In his article for Fansided, Adam Cheek referred to the sixth-place all-time saves leader as follows: "He is the left-handed National League complement to Mariano Rivera and was as dominant of a closer as you can find." What Braves' reliever was Cheek referring to?

Answer: Billy Wagner played and starred in relief for one year with the Braves and captured the division title. At age thirty-eight, he could still deliver a ninety-eight-mph fastball that he threw for the final pitch to capture his 400th save in July 2010.

299. He became the first pitcher in MLB history to produce a sub-1.00 ERA over at least seventy appearances. Who is this Braves lefty?

Answer: Eric O'Flaherty posted a 0.98 earned run average in seventy-eight games in 2011. The lefty followed that season with a 1.73 ERA over sixty-four appearances in 2012.

300. One of the most controversial calls on the field of play occurred on October 5, 2012, during a one-game Wild Card Playoff to decide who would win the NLDS. Can you describe the event?

Answer: True to its name, the Wild Card playoff game between the Atlanta Braves and the St. Louis Cardinals got wild in the bottom of the eighth inning when the umpires invoked the infield fly rule on a fly ball to left field off the bat of Andrelton Simmons that had seemingly dropped for a hit (or an error). The problem with the call was the ball was hit ninety feet out into the outfield, not in the area of the infield. The call by the umpires killed the Atlanta rally and the chances of the Braves winning the contest. This highly controversial call sent Brave fans into a hot-dog-and-beer-throwing frenzy never before seen in Atlanta sports.

301. Bobby Cox set a number of records acting as manager for the Braves between 1978 and 1981 and 1990-2010. What is one record he set that most baseball experts agree will never be broken?

Answer: Bobby Cox holds the all-time record for ejections in Major League Baseball with 158 (plus an additional three postseason ejections), a record previously held by John McGraw. Unlike McGraw, Cox did not have a reputation for a fiery temper, and Cox generally only got ejected to prevent his players from being ejected.

302. What premier high school athlete struggling with anxiety and drug abuse walked away from a scholarship at Texas A.M. to spend four years wandering the Western United States before returning to baseball?

Answer: After four years of soul-searching and finding himself, Evan

Gattis returned to baseball, and was drafted by the Braves in 2010. He made the team's Opening Day roster in 2013. Gattis, nicknamed "El Oso Blanco" or "The White Bear" due to his raw power, hit twenty-one homers in 105 games and placed seventh in the Rookie of the Year voting.

303. His home run total is the most ever by a National League switch hitter. Who is this slugger that delivered long balls from both sides of the plate?

Answer: Chipper Jones' 468 home runs are the most ever by a National League switch hitter.

304. The Atlanta Braves recently started a between-innings promotion called "Beat the Freeze," where a spectator is given an enormous head start in a race on the outfield warning track from foul post to foul post and is then chased down by a blue spandex-wearing sprinter—the Freeze. Who is this entertaining speed demon?

Answer: Nigel Talton is the Freeze. He has been a member of the Atlanta Braves' ground crew for eight years. He was a sprinter at Kennesaw State and in 2011 notched a 4.28-second forty at a football camp, a time just six one-hundredths of a second slower than John Ross's all-time NFL combine record. Talton's races have rung up millions of views on Facebook and Twitter. What started out as an ad skit for Racetrack gas station has turned into a successful marketing promotion, while making Talton a national celebrity. He paints the baselines before the game and then heads off to race fans in the outfield during the game.

305. Can you name the ten players with retired numbers for the Braves? Please put them in the correct order of retirement?

Answer: Warren Spahn (21), Eddie Mathews (41), Hank Aaron (44), Phil Niekro (35). Dale Murphy (3), Greg Maddux (31), Tom Glavine (47), Bobby Cox (6), John Smoltz (29), and Chipper Jones (10).

306. On January 8, 2014, what two members of the 1995 Braves World Champions were voted into Baseball's Hall of Fame in their first year of eligibility?

Answer: Greg Maddux was the first pitcher to win four consecutive Cy Young Awards, winning three with the Braves. In those four years, his ERA was 1.98. As of 2014, in addition to winning a record eighteen Gold Gloves, he was the only pitcher to ever win fifteen games in seventeen seasons. Tom Glavine also won two Cy Young Awards. Glavine won twenty games five times. Glavine helped steer the Braves to the 1995 World Series championship with a one-hit shutout in game six. Maddux was named on 97.2% of HOF ballots, while Glavine was named on almost ninety-two percent.

307. Who was this Cooperstown Hall of Famer that became the fourth announcer to be inducted into the Braves Hall of Fame?

Answer: Don Sutton pitched in MLB for twenty-three seasons and posted a 324-256 record. After retiring from baseball, Sutton was an analyst for the Atlanta Braves for twenty-eight seasons, calling games on both television and radio. "We are deeply saddened by the passing of our dear friend, Don Sutton," the Braves said in a statement after his death. "A generation of Braves fans came to know his voice ... Don was as feared on the mound as he was beloved in the booth. Don brought an unmatched knowledge of the game and his sharp wit to his calls. But despite all the success, Don never lost his generous character or humble personality."

308. Who was the last Major League Baseball general manager to enter the Baseball Hall of Fame?

Answer: John Schuerholz was inducted into the MLB Hall of Fame as the general manager of the Braves to which he served in that position from 1990 to 2007. Afterward, he was the acting Braves President from 2007 to 2016.

309. Three extremely talented Braves players were signed coming from Curacao of the Dutch West Indies. Can you name the three players, two of which won Gold Gloves and one who won the Silver Slugger?

Answer: Andruw Jones was the third player ever signed from Curacao. He won ten Gold Gloves and is a four-time all-star. Andrelton Simmons won two Gold Gloves for Atlanta. Ozzie Albies was the fifteenth signing from Curacao. He is a two-time All-Star and won the Silver Slugger representing the Braves.

310. This Brave has been hailed as one of the best three switch hitters to ever play in the Major Leagues. Can you name him and the other two who excelled from both sides of the plate?

Answer: Chipper Jones~Atlanta Braves (468 HR, 2726 Hits, .303 Avg.), Eddie Murray~Baltimore Orioles (504 HR, 3255 Hits, .287 Avg.), and Mickey Mantle~ New York Yankees (536 HR, 2414 Hits, .298 Avg.).

311. What MLB number one draft pick hit an inside-the-park home run for his first Big League four-bagger?

Answer: Dansby Swanson stroked an inside-the-park home run against Washington on September 6, 2016. It was Atlanta's first such home run since 2001. With the four-bagger, Swanson followed Paul Runge as only the second Braves player to ever make an inside-the-park home run with his first career Big-League home run.

312. Who was the first skipper to receive the Manager of the Year in both the American and National Leagues?

Answer: In 1991, Bobby Cox became the first manager to win the award in both leagues. He was honored for his leadership with the Atlanta Braves and had previously won with the Toronto Blue Jays in 1985. The following managers have accomplished the extraordinary feat since Cox: Tony La Russa, Lou Piniella, Jim Leyland, Bob Melvin, Davey Johnson, and Joe Maddon.

313. Who was this Brave that Baseball America rated the number one baseball prospect for Major League Baseball on his eighteenth birthday in 2018?

Answer: Ronald Acuna's highly anticipated premiere for his rookie season didn't disappoint. The rising star from Curacao was especially strong during the second half of the 2018 season, where he hit .322 with nineteen homers. From July 31 to Aug. 15, Acuna tallied a league-best nine homers. Acuna's eight leadoff home runs are a Braves franchise record. For his efforts, Acuna won the Rookie of the Year Award.

314. Who was the youngest Brave to hit two grand slams?

Answer: Ozzie Albies was a starter in the Braves' Opening Day lineup of the 2018 season. On June 12, 2018, Albies hit a grand slam against the New York Mets en route to an 8-2 win and subsequently became the youngest player (age twenty-one) ever to have two grand slams. On June 25, 2018, Albies hit his first career walk-off home run against the Cincinnati Reds. Albies clouted twenty-four home runs in the 2018 season.

315. In 2018, Ronald Acuna became the eighth Braves player to win Rookie of the Year honors and the first since Craig Kimbrel won in 2011. Can you name the other six?

Answer: Alvin Dark (1948), Sam Jethroe (1950), Earl Williams (1971), Bob Horner (1978), David Justice (1990), and Rafael Furcal (2000).

316. What Braves manager received Manager of the Year honors in only his second full year managing in the Big Leagues?

Answer: Brian Snitker has been in the Braves' organization in a variety of roles since becoming a minor league player in 1977. He became their manager in 2016. On November 13, 2018, after his second full season at the helm, Snitker was named the *Sporting News* National League Manager of the Year, which he shared with Craig Counsell of the Milwaukee Brewers.

317. The Braves are the first team in MLB history to have two players under age twenty-two make the All-Star team. Can you name the two?

Answer: Mike Soroka being selected for the 2019 National League All-Star team makes him the youngest pitcher in franchise history to achieve the honor. The twenty-one-year-old starter joins Ronald Acuna, also twenty-one.

318. The Waffle House has 2100 locations in America. Can you name the location of the only one that serves beer?

Answer: Do you want to enjoy your scattered and covered hash browns with a cold beer. If so, you will need to take a seat in the Waffle House in Truist Park. It is the only WH restaurant located in a Major League stadium in America, and just another reason Truist Park is such a fun place to visit.

319. What three Braves won the Silver Slugger Award in 2019?

Answer: The award is given to the best hitter at his position. The Braves led all teams in both leagues with three winners. Ozzie Albies and teammates Ronald Acuna Jr. and Freddie Freeman won the 2019 National League Silver Slugger Awards for second base, outfield, and first base, respectively.

Ozzie Albies: The five-foot-eight spark plug improved his batting statistics in every category. He sported a .295 batting average coupled with 102 runs scored, 189 hits, a career-high twenty-four home runs, eighty-six RBIs, fifteen stolen bases, forty-three doubles, and eight triples.

Ronald Acuna Jr. had an All-Star sophomore season that placed him fifth in the MVP voting. He racked up forty-one home runs, 175 hits, and led the league with thirty-seven stolen bases, and 127 runs scored.

Freddie Freeman: In his tenth season with the Braves, the six-foot-five first baseman's statistics remain rock solid and consistent with his numbers throughout his career. In 597 at-bats, Freeman produced: 176 hits, 121 RBIs, crossed the plate 113 times, stole six bases, hit at a .295 clip, and slugged a career-high thirty-eight home runs. His on-base percentage of .389 and .549 slugging percentage were career highs.

320. Who is Mike Plant?

Answer: As an integral part of the Atlanta Braves executive leadership team, Plant played a critical role in the Braves' efforts to secure and plan Truist Park (formerly Suntrust Park) and the contiguous mixed-use development, The Battery Atlanta. Plant joined the Braves organization in November 2003 as executive vice president of business operations. He is serving in his sixth season as president of development.

321. Terry McGuirk is chairman of the board for the Atlanta Braves. What has been his involvement with the franchise for the last twenty years?

Answer: Terry McGuirk became the CEO for the Braves in 2001. Before joining the organization, he was CEO for the Turner Broadcasting System from 1996 to 2001.

322. Only four players in MLB have finished the season with forty home runs and forty stolen bases to their credit. What Braves player fell three stolen bases short of becoming the fifth?

Answer: In his second season with the Braves, Ronald Acuna Jr. finished three stolen bases short of being only the fifth player in the history of MLB to qualify for the forty home runs and forty stolen bases club. The four members of the forty-forty club are Alfonso Soriano of the Nationals, 2006, Alex Rodriguez of the Mariners, 1998, Barry Bonds of the Giants, 1996, and Jose Canseco of the A's, 1988.

323. On September 10, 2020, the Braves broke a ninety-one-year-old record set by St. Louis Cardinals for runs scored in a game. How many did they push across the plate?

Answer: Adam Duvall hit a bases-loaded home run in the seventh inning to bring the Braves' run count to twenty-nine, eclipsing the total of the twenty-eight set by the Cardinals in a 28-6 romp over the Phillies in 1929.

324. What former Brave holds the record for consecutive games without committing an error?

Answer: Nick Markakis had not made an error in 398 games. His streak stretched back to August 10, 2012, while playing for the Orioles. The sure-handed right fielder committed his first miscue while playing for the Braves on June 25, 2015. After a base hit was hit his way, he bobbled the ball, allowing the runner to advance to second, ending his errorless streak

325. In 2021 Dansby Swanson became the first shortstop since 1964 to hit twenty or more home runs. Who was his predecessor?

Answer: Shortstop Denis Menke hit twenty homers in 1964, joining four other teammates that equaled or exceeded that number: Joe Torre (20), Eddie Mathews (23), Rico Carty (22), and Hank Aaron (24). Menke played for the Braves in Milwaukee and Atlanta from 1962 to 1967.

326. The 2021 Atlanta Braves fell three home runs shy of accomplishing a feat that had never occurred in MLB. What was it?

Answer: Never in the history of MLB had four infielders on the same team hit thirty or more home runs in the same season. The Braves quartet came close with the following longball numbers: Freddie Freeman (31), Ozzie Albies (30), Austin Riley (33), and Dansby Swanson (27). The Braves are just the second team in MLB history to have four infielders hit twenty-five or more four-baggers during the same season.

327. Can you name the three managers inducted to the Hall of Fame on July 27, 2014?

Answer: Bobby Cox (2504-2001), Tony LaRussa (2821-2434), and Joe Torre (2326-1997).

328. Who hit the longest ball for the Braves since Statcast began tracking distance in 2015?

Answer: Ronald Acuna's mammoth 495-foot moonshot against the Boston Red Sox in September 2020 holds that record.

329. On September 2, 2020, two Atlanta ballplayers accomplished a feat that had never been done before in MLB. Who were these two sluggers, and what did they do to set the record?

Answer: When Marcel Ozuna hit three home runs on September 1, 2020 and Adam Duvall followed on September 2 also hitting three out of the park, they became the first pair of teammates to connect for three-homer games on back-to-back days. Both games were against the Boston Red Sox at Fenway Park.

330. What four-time All-Star had not hit a grand slam home run in his first 1,383 career games and then hit two in three days?

Answer: On September 4, 2020, Freddie Freeman came up for the 105th time with the bases loaded. The Brave slugger had never hit a grand slam homer in the Majors. In the second game of a doubleheader against the Washington Nationals, Freeman hit the first of his career off of pitcher Tanner Rainey. Two days later, he hit another grand slam, against National pitcher Kyle Finnegan.

331. There is no person dead or alive that has attended more Atlanta Braves games than this popular employee. Who is this individual who would always greet you at the ballpark with a smile and a story?

Answer: Walter Banks, at eighty-two years old, served the Atlanta Braves as an usher, greeter, and ambassador in three stadiums for his fifty-six-year career. His first two games working for the franchise were exhibition games between Milwaukee and Detroit, played April 9-11, 1965. He still has his $9.47 check for working the two contests. Over his tenure as usher and spokesman for the Braves, he has worked over 8,000 games to the delight of countless fans.

332. In 2020 D.J. LeMathieu (.364 batting average) and Luke Voit (22 home runs) of the New York Yankees became the first players to lead their league in batting average and home runs since two Braves accomplished this in 1959. Can you name them?

Answer: For the 1959 season, Hank Aaron captured the batting title (.355), collecting a league-leading 223 hits, and Eddie Mathews banged out forty-six homers.

333. Max Fried tied a hundred-year-old record held by Babe Ruth. What was the Babe's record while pitching for the Boston Red Sox?

Answer: Fried tied the record when he collected his sixth win and led the Braves to a perfect 8-0 record in his first eight starts for the season. Ruth set the mark in 1917 with the Red Sox when his team won the first eight games he appeared in that season.

334. Who was the National League's first recipient of the Designated Hitter Award in 2020?

Answer: Marcel Ozuna won the award for his outstanding performance. In the Covid-19 shortened season, he led the league with eighteen home runs, fifty-six RBIs, and 145 total bases.

335. Winning two in a row never seemed so challenging. What record did Atlanta set concerning back-to-back wins in 2021?

Answer: Atlanta alternated losses and wins for seventeen games, an MLB record.

336. Why did Major League Baseball pull the 2021 All-Star Game out of Atlanta?

Answer: The 2021 Midsummer Classic scheduled for Atlanta was canceled due to the opposition to Georgia's new restrictive voting law.

337. Major League Baseball pulled the 2021 All-Star Game out of Atlanta. Can you name the other Midsummer Classic scheduled for the Braves franchise that was canceled?

Answer: This 1953 game was initially scheduled for Braves Field in Boston, which had hosted the All-Star Game in 1936. When the Braves made their unexpected announcement of their relocation to Milwaukee in mid-March, the game was awarded to Cincinnati and played at Crosley Field.

150 Years of Braves Trivia

338. Who was the first pinch hitter who hit for the cycle on only five pitches?

Answer: Eddie Rosario hit for the cycle with Atlanta on September 19, 2021. The notorious first-ball hitter connected for a single, double, triple, and home run after being served up only five pitches in four at-bats.

339. In 2018, what Braves ROY was the first rookie to lead his team in home runs since another first year player did so in 1930?

Answer: Ronald Acuna's season was historic. He was the first rookie to lead a Braves team in home runs since 1930 when the first year sensation Wally Berger clouted thirty-eight long balls to lead his team. Ronald Acuna Jr. had impressive rookie numbers over 111 games, including 127 hits, twenty-seven home runs, twenty-six doubles, sixteen stolen bases, and a .293 batting average.

340. Can you name the six Braves players to win the National League MVP award?

Answer: Johnny Evers (1914), Hank Aaron (1957), Dale Murphy (1982 and 1983), Terry Pendleton (1991), Chipper Jones (1999), and Freddie Freeman (2020).

341. "Twelve Years, Six Months, Twenty-Five Days: A Long Journey Back to the Majors." New York Times. After playing one year for the San Diego Padres in 2008, what player stuck with it in the minors for 4,589 days for the opportunity to play in the Major League again?

Answer: After a long wait, Sean Kazmar Jr. was brought up for a couple of games to fill in for the Braves. Before being sent back down to the minors, Kazmar had two at-bats. His story is essential as his career demonstrates a player's stick-to-itiveness and love for the game.

342. In the World Championship season, the Miracle Braves used twelve pitchers. How many did the World Champion Braves employ in 2021? Was the number 15, 25, 35, or 45?

Answer: Manager Brian Snitker and pitching coach Rick Kranitz used forty-five pitchers throughout the 2021 season.

343. This player was key in helping Atlanta punch its ticket to the 2021 World Series. Who was this player that was the Most Valuable Player in the NLCS?

Answer: Eddie Rosario was awarded the NLCS MVP award for his performance in the series. The mid-season acquisition stroked fourteen hits in twenty-five at-bats, with three home runs and nine RBIs.

344. This player joined the Braves roster in July 2021. Can you name this recipient of the 2021 World Series MVP award?

Answer: Jorge Soler became the second Cuban-born player to win the award after he helped Atlanta capture its first World Series title in twenty-six years.

345. In their 150-year history, the Braves have captured eighteen National League pennants. What three teams have won more?

Answer: Los Angeles Dodgers (24), San Francisco Giants (23), and the St Louis Cardinals (19).

346. Bill McKechnie, Billy Southworth, Casey Stengel, Joe Torre, Tony LaRussa, Bobby Cox. Which of these Hall of Fame managers did not wear a uniform as a player for the Braves?

Answer: Bobby Cox never played for the Braves. He played third base for the New York Yankees during the 1968 and 1969 seasons. The others played for the Braves: McKechnie (1913), Southworth (1921-1923), Stengel (1924-1925), Torre (1960-1968), and LaRussa (1971).

347. For the first time in the team's franchise history, two Braves hit for the cycle (single, double, triple, and home run) in the same season. Can you name the two that touched all the bases in 2021?

Answer: Freddie Freeman and Eddie Rosario.

348. What three Atlanta players won the Roberto Clemente Award, and why was it created?

Answer: Phil Niekro, Dale Murphy, and John Smoltz have won the Roberto Clemente Award. In 1973, this award for charitable contributions was established in honor of the legendary Hall of Famer, who died in a plane crash on December 31, 1972, while on a humanitarian mission to assist earthquake victims in Nicaragua.

349. Can you name the three number-one picks in the MLB draft who started their careers with the Atlanta Braves?

Answer: Bob Horner, Chipper Jones, and Dansby Swanson. Horner was drafted number one in 1978 out of Arizona State University, where he set a then-NCAA record of fifty-eight career home runs. Jones had accepted a scholarship offer to play college baseball at the University of Miami when he was drafted. Swanson was a finalist for the 2015 Golden Spikes Award, presented annually to the nation's top college player. He was drafted by Arizona and traded to the Braves in the off season.

350. In the 150 years of the Braves franchise, seven of the organization's managers have been inducted into the Baseball Hall of Fame. How many can you name?

Answer: Harry Wright (1872-1881), Frank Selee (1890-1901), Bill McKechnie (1930-1937), Casey Stengel (1938-1943), Billy Southworth (1946-1951), and Bobby Cox (1978-1981, 1990-2010). Wright was inducted as a player.

351. Thirty-two individuals have won more than one MVP award in their careers, including thirteen who've won in back-to-back seasons. Of those, only two are still active. Of the eleven retired winners of consecutive year MVP awards not associated with steroid use, can you name the two not in the Baseball Hall of Fame?

Answer: Dale Murphy and Roger Maris.

352. Who was the only player to represent the Braves in three American cities that his ball club called home?

Answer: Over a fifteen-year stretch, Eddie Matthews played in three franchise cities, Boston (1952), Milwaukee (1953-1965), and Atlanta (1966).

References

Atlanta Braves: The First 25 Years.
Atlanta Constitution
The Atlanta Journal
Atlanta Magazine
Babe: The Legend Comes to Life by Robert W. Creamer
The Ballplayers edited by Mike Shatzkin
Bleacher Report/Atlanta Braves
The Ballplayers edited by Mike Shatzkin
The Baseball Chronology edited by James Charlton
The Baseball Encyclopedia Joseph L. Reichler, editor
Baseball Registers by the Sporting News
Baseball's Greatest Quotations by Paul Dickson
Boston American
The Boston Braves by Harold Kaese
Boston Globe
Boston Herald
Boston Post
Braves media guides
Braves yearbooks
The Braves: Pick and the Shovel by Al Hirshberg
Caught Short by Donald Davidson with Jesse Outlar
Chop Talk
The Complete Baseball Record Book by The Sporting News
Eddie Mathews and the National Pastime by Eddie Mathews and Bob Buege.
The Great All-Time Baseball Record Book, Joseph L. Richler, editor; revised by Ken Samuelson.
The Milwaukee Braves: A Baseball Eulogy by Bob Buege.
Milwaukee Journal
Milwaukee Sentinel
Miracle in Atlanta by Furman Bisher
National Baseball Hall of Fame and Museum Yearbook
The National Baseball Library and Archive at Cooperstown, New York
National League Green Book
The New York Times
The Sporting News
Sport Magazine
Sports Illustrated
Tomahawk
Wikipedia

Web Site Resources

www.ajc.com
www. baseball-almanac.com
www. baseballanaylysts.com
www.baseballdigest.com
www.baseballindex.com
www. baseballhall.org
www. baseball-reference.com
www.bizjournals.com
www.bleacherreport.com
www.boston.com
www.braves.com
www.brittannica.com
www.bronxbanter.com
www.collection.baseball.com
www.espn.com
www.forbes.com
www.funtrivia.com
www.hardballtimes.com
www.mlb.com
www.newspapers.com
www.newyorktimes.com
www.sabr.com
www.sporacle.com
www.sportingnews.com
www.sportsillustrated.com
www.sportsjournalism.com
www.talkingchop.com
www.tomahawktake.com
www.youtube.com
www.washingtonpost.com
www.wikipedia.com

Photo Credits

Cover~ Baseball Image-Courtesy of Brian J. Matis Photography
Inside Front Cover-Tom Glavine- Courtesy of REUTERS/Alamy
Felipe Alou- Courtesy of RLFE Pix/Alamy
Hank Aaron 715- Courtesy of Everett Collection Historical/Alamy
Atlanta Fulton County Stadium- Courtesy of Age Fotostock/Alamy
Eddie Rosario, Travis d' Arnaud- Courtesy of UPI/Alamy
Fredd Tenny, Herman Long, Bobby Lowe & Jimmy Collins- Michael T. "Nuf Ced" McGreevy Collection, Boston Public Library
Johnny Sain- Courtesy of Boston Public Library, Leslie Jones Collection
Fred Haney- Courtesy of Wisconsin Historical Society
Dedication~ Henry Aaron~ Aaron looking back- Courtesy of the National Baseball Hall of Fame, Aaron at-bat- Everett Collection, Inc./Alamy
Boston~ King Kelly- Michael T. "Nuf Ced" McGreevy Collection, Boston Public Library
Harry Wright~ Courtesy of the National Baseball Hall of Fame/Public Domain
King Kelly~ Michael T. "Nuf Ced" McGreevy Collection, Boston Public Library
John Clarkson~Courtesy of Courtesy of the National Baseball Hall of Fame Library
Hugh Duffy~ Michael T. "Nuf Ced" McGreevy Collection, Boston Public Library
Frank Selee~ Courtesy of the National Baseball Hall of Fame Library/Public Domain
1914 Miracle Braves~ Courtesy of the Sporting News Collection/Public Domain
Rabbit Maranville~ Courtesy of the Boston Public Library, Leslie Jones Collection
Braves Field~ Courtesy of the Boston Public Library, Leslie Jones Collection
Bill McKechnie~ Courtesy of the Boston Public Library, Leslie Jones Collection
Wally Berger~ Courtesy of the Boston Public Library, Leslie Jones Collection
Casey Stengel~ Courtesy of the Boston Public Library, Leslie Jones Collection
Billy Southworth~ Courtesy of the National Baseball Hall of Fame
Spahn and Sain~ Courtesy of the Boston Public Library, Leslie Jones Collection
Lolly Hopkins~ Courtesy of the Boston Public Library, Leslie Jones Collection
Jackie Robinson and Sam Jethro~ Courtesy of the Boston Public Library, Leslie Jones Collection
Milwaukee Newspaper~ Courtesy of the Robert Kohler Collection
Billy Bruton/Warren Spahn~ Courtesy of the David Klug Collection
Sibby Sisti~ Courtesy of the Boston Public Library, Leslie Jones Collection
Lulu Gibson~ Courtesy of the Robert Kohler Collection
Bobby Thomson and Hank Aaron~ Courtesy of the Milwaukee County Historical Society
Eddie Mathews~ Courtesy of the Robert Kohler Collection
Mathews, Adcock 4-fingers, and Pafko~ The David Klug Collection
Fred Haney and Casey Stengel~ Courtesy of the Wisconsin Historical Society
Lou Burdette~ Courtesy of the David Klug Collection
Warren Spahn and Hank Aaron~ Courtesy of the David Klug Collection
Wes Covington~ Courtesy of the Wisconsin Historical Society
Gold Glove-Hank Aaron~ Carmen K. Sisson/Cloudybright/Alamy

Harvey Haddix/Joe Adcock~ Courtesy of the David Klug Collection
Win or Lose- We Love Our Braves~ Courtesy of the David Klug Collection.
Juan Marichal and Warren Spahn~ Both photos are eligible for use by Public Domain
Eddie Mathews~Courtesy of the Wisconsin Historical Society
Warren Spahn~ Courtesy of the Wisconsin Historical Society
Mathews and Aaron walking up tunnel~ Courtesy of Milwaukee County Historical Society
Hank Aaron 715~ Courtesy of CSU Archives/Everett Collection/Alamy
Mayor Ivan Allen Jr., Governor Carl Sanders~ Courtesy of Carl Sanders family
Tony Cloninger~ Courtesy of The Topps Company, Inc.
Felipe Alou~ Courtesy of RFLE Pix/Alamy
Announcer Ernie Johnson Sr.~ ZUMA Press, Inc./ Alamy
Rico Carty~ Wikipedia/Pubic Domain
Satchel Paige with the Braves~ the Atlanta History Center
Bill Lucas and Bobby Cox~ Courtesy of the Atlanta Journal Constitution
A Young Bob Horner~ Courtesy of the Atlanta Journal Constitution
Gene Garber/Pete Rose~ Courtesy of the Atlanta Journal Constitution
Hank Aaron/ Back Cover~ Courtesy of the National Baseball Hall of Fame
Opening night Braves Invitation~ Courtesy of Susie Hayes Kyle
Dale Murphy~ Courtesy of the Atlanta Journal Constitution
All-Century Team~ Courtesy of REUTERS/Alamy
Greg Maddux~ Courtesy of REUTERS/Alamy
John Smoltz~ Courtesy of REUTERS/Alamy
Andruw Jones~ Courtesy of REUTERS/Alamy
Jeff Francoeur ~ Courtesy of REUTERS/Alamy
Paul Synder and Bobby Cox~ Courtesy of the Atlanta Journal Constitution
Simpson, Sutton, Van Wieren, and Caray~ Courtesy of the Atlanta Journal Constitution
Bobby Cox- Courtesy of UPI/Alamy
Chipper Jones~ Courtesy of the Atlanta Journal Constitution
Bobby Cox~ Courtesy of REUTERS/Alamy
Ronald Acuna, Jr.~ Courtesy of Austin McAfee/Alamy
Brian Snitker~ UPI/Alamy
Freddie Freeman~ Courtesy of the Atlanta Journal Constitution
Sean Kazmar, Jr.~ Courtesy of Bernie Connelly
Back Cover-Thanks Bobby- Courtesy of ZUMA Press, Inc./Alamy
Chipper Jones- Courtesy of the Atlanta Journal Constitution
Eddie Mathews- Courtesy of the Wisconsin Historical Society
John Clarkson- Courtesy of the National Baseball Hall of Fame
Phil Niekro- Courtesy of Everett Collection Historical/Alamy

Index

A

Aaron, Hank, 18, 41, 42, 44, 45, 46, 47, 49, 50, 51, 52, 53, 54, 57, 58, 64, 65, 66, 67, 68, 70, 71, 72, 75, 84, 88, 92, 101, 107, 109, 110
Aaron, Tommy, 75
Acuna, Ronald, Jr., 34, 103, 104, 105, 106, 107, 110
Adams, Babe, 47
Adcock, Joe, 40, 41, 43, 51, 52, 53, 65, 71
Alexander, Doyle, 77
Alexander, Grover Cleveland, 17
All-Star game, 27, 29, 44, 65, 70, 109
All-Star team, 1934, 27
Albies, Ozzie, 102, 103, 105, 107
Alexander Doyle, 77
Allen, Ivan Jr., 59
Allen, Dick, 66
Allen, Lee, 26
Alou, Felipe, 60, 90
Alou, Jesus, 60, 61
Alou, Matty, 60
America's Team, 67
Atlanta Braves, 14, 63, 67, 81, 82, 113
Atlanta Braves Foundation, 71
Atlanta Falcons, 82
Atlanta-Fulton County Stadium, 59, 60, 64, 73, 83
Avery, Steve, 79, 80, 81, 96

B

Banks, Walter, 108
Bartholomay, Bill, 64
Barrett, Red, 31
Baseball Hall of Fame, 57, 61, 64, 74, 78, 84, 94, 101, 112
Battery Atlanta, 105
Battle of the Bulge, 31
Beatles, The, 64
Beat the Freeze, 100
Belinda, Stan, 82

Berger, Wally, 28, 29, 34, 110
Berkman, Lance, 94
Berra, Yogi, 46
Betemit, William, 94
Birmingham, Joe, 21
Blauser, Jeff, 87, 96
Blyleven, Bert, 68
Bond, Tommy, 12, 13
Bonds, Barry, 82, 106
Boston Beaneaters, 11, 12, 14, 16, 18, 19, 20, 38
Boston Bees, 13, 29, 30
Boston Braves, 9, 12, 13, 20, 21, 22, 23, 24, 25, 28, 31, 34, 35, 37, 39, 70, 113
Boston Celtics, 49
Boston Doves, 13, 20
Boston Red Caps, 11, 12, 13, 38
Boston Red Sox, 36, 39, 109
Boston Rustlers, 13, 20
Boston Red Stockings, 11, 13
Boyer, Clete, 65, 98
Boyer, Clyod, 65
Boyer, Ken, 65
Braves Field, 23, 24, 29
Braves Hall of Fame, 19, 43, 75
Bream, Sid, 81
Brock, Lou, 14
Brooklyn Dodgers, 24
Brooklyn Robbins, 24
Brouthers, Dan, 79
Brown College, 14
Bruton, Bill, 40, 42, 43, 45
Burdette, Lou, 47, 48, 51, 52, 53
Burke, Chris, 94

C

Cabrera, Francisco, 82
Cadore, Leon, 24
Candiotti, Tom, 55
Candlestick Park, 60
Canseco, Jose, 106
Canton Bulldogs, 24

Cantwell, Ben, 29
Capra, Buzz, 67
Caray, Skip, 97
Carty, Rico, 63, 66, 107
Cepeda, Orlando, 65
Chamberlain, Icebox, 17
Chambers Award, 23
Chambliss, Chris,
Cheek, Adam, 98
Chief Noc-A-Homa, 61
Chicago Cubs, 29
Cincinnati Reds, 17, 31, 53
Cincinnati Red Legs, 10
Chicago White Stockings, 13
Cincinnati Red Stockings, 11
Clark, Will, 95
Clarkson, John, 15, 16
Clemens, Roger, 89
Clemente, Roberto, 50, 66
Cleveland Indians, 46, 88
Cloninger, Tony, 57, 60
College Baseball Hall of Fame, 72, 95
College World Series, 95
Collins, Jimmy, 14, 15
Covington Wes, 42, 48
Cobb, Ty, 23, 43
Cooley, Duff, 76
Conley, Gene, 45, 49, 96
Conrad, Brooks, 97
Counsell, Craig, 104
Cox, Bobby, 89, 90, 97, 99, 101, 103, 107, 111
Crandall, Del, 45, 52
Crawford, Carl, 80
Cy Young Award, 37, 53, 78, 81, 83, 87, 90, 91, 93, 101

D

Dark, Alvin, 34, 54, 75, 104
Davis, Tommy, 54
Davidson, Donald, 45
Designated Hitter Award, 109

Devers, Rafael, 95
Devine, Joey, 94
Dressen, Chuck, 52
Drew, John, 91
Drysdale, Don, 18, 61
Duffy, Hugh, 16, 17, 18, 33
Duvall, Adam, 106, 107

E

Easter, Luke, 71
Eckersley, Dennis, 92
Elliott, Bob, 32
Evans, Darrel, 66
Evers, Johnny, 20, 22, 23, 110

F

Feller, Bob, 37
Fenway Park, 107
Fette, Lou, 29
Finnegan, Kyle, 108
Fonda, Jane, 80
Ford Frick Award, 76
Ford, Whitey, 37, 46
Fort Benning, 30
Francis, Earl, 55
Francoeur, Jeff, 92, 93, 94
Freeman, Freddie, 97, 105, 107, 108, 110, 112
Freeze, the, 100
Frick, Ford, 51
Fried, Max, 109
Frisbee Night, 75
Fuchs, Emil, 26, 29
Furcal, Rafael, 34, 91, 93, 104

G

Gaffney, James, 20
Galarraga, Andres, 88
Galvin, Pud, 78
Garber, Gene, 69
Gant, Ron,

Garr, Ralph, 66, 72
Gattis, Evan, 99, 100
Gautreau, Doc, 25
Gehrig, Lou, 88
Gibson, Bob, 89, 98
Glavine, Tom, 75, 78, 79, 81, 85, 87, 90, 95, 96, 101
Gold Glove Award, 45, 49, 50, 63, 65, 71, 78, 94, 101, 102
Gooden, Dwight, 98
Gowdy, Hank, 21, 30
Green, Pumpsie, 37
Green, Shawn, 43
Greene, Tommy, 79
Grimm, Charlie, 45

H

Haddix, Harvey, 50
Hall, Albert, 76
Hamilton, Billy, 14
Haney, Fred, 45, 46
Hayes, Jr., Arthur, III, IV, V, 125
Hayes, Bradsher, 125
Hazle, Bob, 45
Heavenly Twins, 18
Henderson, Ricky, 80
Hiller, Chuck, 52
Hopkins, Lolly, 36
Holiday, Roy, 95
Holmes, Tommy, 32, 33
Hope, Bob, 75
Horner, Bob, 34, 68, 77, 95, 98, 104, 112
Hornsby, Rogers, 26, 32, 88
House, Tom, 56
Hubbell, Carl 30, 53
Hudson, Tim, 95
Human Crab, 20, 21
Hundley, Todd,"Hot Rod". 91

J

James, Bill, 22, 23
Jethroe, Sam, 34, 36, 38, 104

Johnson Dave, 66, 103
Johnson, Ernie, 62
Johnson, Kelly, 92, 94
Johnson, Randy, 72, 88
Johnson, Walter, 74, 78
Jones, Andrux, 88, 92, 94, 102
Jones, Chipper, 41, 84, 85, 87, 88, 96, 98, 100, 101, 102, 110, 112
Jordan, Brian, 96
Jury Box,
Justice, David, 34, 81, 82, 86, 96, 104

K

Kaline, Kaline, 49
Kasmar, Sean, 111
Kauffman, Mark, 44
Kelly, Mike, "King", 11, 13, 14, 79
Kieschnick, Brooks, 95
Kimbrell, Craig, 34, 97, 104
King of the Southern Diamond, 125
Klesko, Ryan, 87
Knucksie, 50, 55
Koufax, Sandy, 18, 44, 61, 89
Kranitz, Rick, 111
Kuiper, Duane, 40

L

La Roche, Adam, 94
La Russa, Tony, 103, 107, 111
Langerhans, Roger, 94
Lemaster, Denny,
LeMathieu, D.J., 108
Lemon Bob, 61
Leibrandt, Charlie, 81
Leyland, Jim, 103
Lockhart, Keith, 87
Lopez, Javy, 87, 88, 91
Logan, Johnny, 32, 40, 45, 98
Long, Herman, 17, 20
Los Angeles Dodgers, 43, 111
Lowe, Bobby, 14, 17, 20
Lucas, Bill, 67, 68, 96

M

McCann, Brian, 92, 94
Maddon, Joe, 103
Maddux, Greg, 12, 75, 83, 87, 88, 90, 98
Mantilla, Felix, 51
Manager of the Year, 104
Mantle, Mickey, 46, 102
Maranville, Rabbit, 22, 23, 25, 28
Marichal, Juan, 54
Maris, Roger, 113
Markakis, Nick, 106
Mathews, Eddie, 36, 37, 40, 43, 44, 46, 49, 51.52, 55, 56, 57, 60, 63, 64, 65, 101, 107
Mathewson, Christy, 17, 25, 48
Maughn, Bill, 50
Mays, Willie, 54, 65
Mazeroski, Bill, 44
Mazzone, Leo, 37
Maddux, Greg, 53, 89, 95, 101
Martinez, J.D., 95
McCarthy, Tommy, 18
McClain, Denny, 37
McCovey, Willie, 64, 65
McGraw, John, 11, 99
McGriff, Fred, 83
McGuirk, Terry, 106
McKechnie, Bill, 27, 111, 112
Melton, Cliff, 30
Melvin, Bob, 103
Menke, Denis, 106, 107
Merker, Kent, 80, 84
Milan, Felix, 63, 65
Millwood, Kevin, 79
Milwaukee Braves. 14, 39, 40, 43, 46, 48, 49, 50, 52, 55, 113
Milwaukee Brewers, 53
Milwaukee County Stadium, 39, 40, 44
Minnesota Twins, 79, 88
Miracle Braves, 21, 38
Montreal Expos, 90
Morrill, John, 11

Morris, Jack,
Mullen, John, 96
Murcer, Bobby, 72
MVP Award, 70, 74, 83
Murphy, Dale, 68, 69, 71, 74, 75, 79, 84, 101, 112, 113
Murray, Eddie, 102, 110
Musial, Stan, 39, 45

N

National League Championship Series, 81
National League Championship Series MVP, 111
National League Division Series, 95
Neagle, Denny, 87
Nehf, Art, 24
New York Giants, 20
New York Mets, 64
New York Yankees, 28, 39, 46, 62, 87, 88, 108
Nichols, Kid, 17, 19
Niekro, Nancy, 71
Niekro, Phil, 44, 50, 53, 55, 64, 69, 71, 72,74. 76, 77, 78, 101, 112
Niekro, Joe, 77
Nixon, Otis, 80, 81

O

Oeschger, Joe, 24, 25, 26
Olympics, 1912, 24
O'Flattery, Eric, 98
O'Rourke, Jim, 11
Ostrich Race, 75
Ozuna, Marcell, 107, 109

P

Pafko, Andy, 40, 43
Paige, Satchel, 35, 64, 65
Peanut Push, 75
Pena, Alejandro, 80

Pendleton, Terry, 83, 110
Perez, Eddie, 87
Perez, Pascual, 74
Perini, Lou, 34, 39
Perry, Gaylord, 32, 77, 79
Perry, Jim, 77
Pershing, General, 30
Philadelphia Athletics, 21
Philadelphia Phillies, 52
Piniella, Lou, 103
Plant, Mike, 105
Polo Grounds, 41, 71
Poole, Jim, 85, 86
President Jimmy Carter, 80

Q

Quinn, Bob, 29

R

Rainey, Tanner, 108
Riley, Austin, 107
Rivera, Mariano, 98
Road Runner, 66
Roberto Clemente, 78
Roberto Clemente Award, 71, 78, 85
Roach, Mel, 40
Roberts, Robin, 53
Robinson, Brooks, 15
Robinson, Jackie, 33, 36, 38, 75
Rodriguez, Alex, 106
Rodriguez, Richard,
Rookie of the Year, 34, 36, 37, 38, 66, 68, 75, 93, 100. 103, 104, 110
Rosario, Eddie, 110, 111, 112
Rose, Pete, 28, 32, 66, 68, 69
Runge, Paul, 102
Ruth, Babe, 9, 14, 27, 28, 32, 33, 67, 70, 84, 88, 109
Ryan, Nolan, 89

S

Sain, Johnny, 33, 34, 35, 38
Saint Louis Browns, 18
Saint Louis Cardinals, 34, 111
San Francisco Giants, 52, 111
Sanders, Carl, 59
Sanders, Deion, 82, 86, 96
Schoendienst, Red, 40, 46, 48, 57
Schuerholz, John,
Scramble for Cash, 75
Schuerholz, John, 101
Seaver, Tom, 62
Selee, Frank, 19, 90, 112
Silver Slugger Award, 92, 102, 105
Simmons, Al, 79
Simmons Andrelton, 102
Simpson, Joe, 97
Sisti, Sibby, 41
Slattery, Jack, 26
Slaughter, Enos Bradsher, 57
Smith, Willie, 64, 86
Smoltz, John, 56, 76, 79, 85, 87,90, 91, 101, 112
Snitker, Brian, 104, 111
Snyder Frank, 24
Snyder, Paul, 96
Soden, Arthur, 20
Soler, Jorge, 111
Soriano, Alfonso, 106
Soroko, Mike, 104
South End Grounds, 35
Southworth, Billy, 34, 55, 111, 112
Spahn, Warren, 12, 31, 34, 35, 37, 39, 40, 46, 47, 52, 53, 54, 55, 56, 57, 61, 80, 81, 89, 93, 101
Spalding, Al, 13
Spehr, Tim, 87
Sports Illustrated, 44, 93
Stallings, George, 22
Stargell, Willie, 60
Stengel, Casey, 30, 46, 111, 112
Stivetts Jack, 15

Super Bowl XXlX, 86
Sutton, Don, 97, 101
Swanson. Dansby, 102, 106, 107, 112

T

Talton, Nigel, 100
Tammany Hall, 20
Tenney, Fred, 14
TBS, 106
The Great Wallenda, 75,
Thomas, Frank, 52
Thomson, Bobby, 42
Thorpe, Jim, 24, 96
Tinker, Joe, 25
Tobin, Jim, 31, 33
Toronto Blue Jays, 80, 88
Torre, Joe, 52, 53, 57, 61, 62, 96, 107, 111
Triple Crown, 17, 54, 72
Truist Park, 105
Turner Broadcasting, 106
Turner, Jim, 29
Turner, Ted, 75, 80

U

Uecker, Bob, 53, 71, 76

V

Ventura, Robin, 95
Voit, Luke, 108

W

Waffle House, 104, 105
Wagner, Billy, 98
Wagner, Onus, 25
Wainwright, Adam, 91
Ward, John Montgomery, 20
Warneke, Lon, 33
Washington, Ron, 125
Westrum, Wes, 44
Wieren, Pete Van, 97
Winfield, Dave, 95

White, Charlie, 42
White, Deacon, 79
Whitney, "Grasshopper" Jim, 12
Wild Card playoff, 99
Wilhelm, Hoyt, 32, 79
Wilson, Jim, 52
Williams, Earl, 34, 104
Williams, Ken, 54
Williams, Marvin, 37
Williams, Ted, 66
Willis, Vic, 19
Wohlers, Mark, 80, 85
World Series, 27, 45, 46, 48, 49, 69, 79, 81, 84, 85, 86, 87, 88
Wrestling Night in the Bullpen, 75
Wright, George, 128
Wright, William H., 9, 10, 11, 112
Wrigley Field, 63

Y

Young, Cy, 32

About Bradsher Hayes

Bradsher Hayes has had a love affair with the Braves for over sixty-two years beginning when at age seven, he and his father would listen to Braves games beginning in 1957, the year the team won the World Series in Milwaukee. His father, from Brooklyn, Massachusetts, had attended the Braves' first World Series with his father for one game in 1914.

Bradsher Hayes is a Southern gentleman and writer who has a deep love for the game of baseball. He is a foremost authority on college and professional baseball at the turn of the twentieth century after years of study and research.

His first work, *King of the Southern Diamond*, was published in the fall of 2019.

He knows baseball and is well paired to the game from his playing time, being a spectator for sixty years and coaching. He played on two state championship baseball teams at Westminster in Atlanta, played college ball at the University of North Carolina, and coached youth programs for ten years. The author has two children, Bo and Jenny, and has been blessed with two grandchildren, Pearl and Olive.

150 Years of the Braves was published in August, 2022. All three books are and available on his websites.

150yearsofthebraves.com & kingofthesoutherndiamond.com

Made in the USA
Las Vegas, NV
22 June 2023

73747588R00069